Praise for Common Ground

In a culture where division is more prevalent than unity, living in harmony with others requires an intentional effort toward peace. *Common Ground* inspires us to restore broken relationships, develop empathy for others, and leverage diverse group skills to advance God's will. In her signature lighthearted and approachable style, Amberly guides us through four sibling relationships from the Bible to uncover obstacles and solutions for loving and living peacefully with others. Armed with an abundance of biblical wisdom and tangible actions, we'll gain the confidence to cultivate unity over conflict.

— **Heather M. Dixon**, speaker and author of *Determined: Living Like Jesus in Every Moment*

What a timely Bible study for a culture that seems so polarized and fragmented. Amberly Neese coaches us through some of the universal land mines that threaten our relationships, encouraging us to take the first step toward common ground.

— **Mary Shannon Hoffpauir**, author of *Lose Control: The Way to Find Your Soul*

As Christians, we need common ground now more than ever! Amberly writes with pinpoint precision, diagnosing the heart of our relational conflicts through powerful biblical insights, humor, and raw vulnerability about her life and relationship struggles. *Common Ground* offers spiritual and practical next steps for growing in Christ together!

— **Barb Roose**, author of *Breakthrough: Finding Freedom in Christ* and
Surrendered: Letting Go and Living Like Jesus

Common Ground takes us directly to the Scriptures. Through the lives of biblical siblings, we find hope and practical wisdom to implement in our own relationships. With her witty style and helpful calls to action, Amberly guides us toward personal growth and the unity desperately needed today within the body of Christ.

—**Melissa Spoelstra**, author of *The Names of God* and other Bible studies and books

COMMON GROUND

Loving Others Despite Our Differences

A STUDY OF SIBLING RIVALRIES IN THE BIBLE

AMBERLY NEESE

Abingdon Women

Nashville

Common Ground

Loving Others Despite Our Differences

ISBN 978-1-7910-1450-6

Contents

About the Author

Amberly Neese

Amberly Neese is a speaker, humorist, and encourager with a passion for "GRINspiring" others. As a featured speaker for the Aspire Women's Events and the main host/comedienne for Marriage Date Night, two popular Christian events that tour nationally, she enjoys touching the hearts and minds and funny bones of people all over the country. The Bible says that laughter is good medicine, and she has found it's also like glue—helping the truths of God's Word to "stick." Amberly loves to remind women of the power and hope found in Scripture. Through a flair for storytelling and a love for Jesus, she candidly opens up her story alongside God's Word to encourage others in their walk with Him.

With a master's degree from Biola University, Amberly serves as an adjunct professor at Grand Canyon University and the Master Connector for Inspiring Growth, an organization developed to equip and encourage growth in leaders and businesses. She is the author of two Bible studies, *Common Ground* and *The Belonging Project*, and one devotional, *The Friendship Initiative*. She and her husband, Scott, have two teenagers and live in Prescott, Arizona, where they enjoy the great outdoors, the Food Network, and all things *Star Wars*.

Follow Amberly:

 @amberlyneese

 @amberlyneese

 @Amberly Neese - Comedian and Speaker

Website   www.amberlyneese.com

Tour information can also be found at marriagedatenight.com and aspirewomensevents.com.

Introduction

Welcome to *Common Ground*! We need only turn on the news or scroll on social media to see overwhelming evidence that we are living in a world of mistrust, misunderstanding, and misconceptions. We face conflict and discord every day, and we need tools to successfully navigate the rough and uncertain waters and live at peace with everyone. How can we honor God, live by our convictions, and find common ground with others despite our differences? We need both biblical and practical wisdom along with proven strategies to love other people well—even the most difficult ones!

Fortunately for us, the Scriptures hold the key to living at peace despite our differences. In this study we will examine some of the sibling rivalries in the Bible and the lessons we can learn from them:

1. Joseph and His Brothers: Combating Jealousy
2. Moses, Miriam, and Aaron: Working Together Despite Differences
3. Mary, Martha, and Lazarus: Appreciating the Contributions of Others
4. Rachel and Leah: Having Compassion for the Plight of Others

Each week as we focus on one story and overarching theme, we will explore a primary Scripture text as well as other related passages to help give us clarity on how we might love one another despite our differences and disagreements. Together, we will dive into how to handle life when, like squabbling siblings, we're struggling to get along. By the way, if you happened to notice that the New Testament characters of Week 3 are sandwiched between Old Testament characters, congratulations! (I wish I had a prize to offer you.) This is simply because I determined to order the weeks according to how their themes build on one another rather than according to placement in the Scriptures.

Each day starts with a Scripture Focus and Today's Key Verses, includes questions and exercises for reflection and application (with space for writing in the book), and ends with a Call to Action. (The lessons are designed to be completed in about twenty minutes.) Then once a week you'll gather with your group to watch a video, discuss what you're learning, and pray together. The session outlines, which provide options for both a 60-minute and a 90-minute session, include discussion questions, activities, prayer prompts, and notes for the video segment. You'll find the outline for each session at the end of the personal lessons for that week.

If you're the facilitator or leader of your group, you'll want to check out the additional leader helps at the back of this book. Ideally, group members should complete the first week of lessons before your first group session. This is because each video message complements the content that you have studied during the week. However, feel free to adapt the study as you wish to meet the needs of your particular group. The questions and activities will guide you in sharing your experiences and learnings together.

My prayer is that even when peace and commonality seem impossible you will be reminded that God is a God of possibilities and reconciliation. His desire is for us to glorify Him in our relationships and to find "common ground" with others, which shapes us to look more like Jesus. Jesus prayed that we would be one just as He is one with God (John 17:21), and when we seek peace and common ground with others, we are part of the answer to that prayer.

Amberly

Week 1

Joseph and His Brothers

Combating Jealousy

Memory Verse

A heart at peace gives life to the body, but envy rots the bones.
(Proverbs 14:30)

Biblical Background

Joseph came from an imperfect family. Like reality TV imperfect.

Joseph's grandparents, Isaac and Rebekah, welcomed twins, Jacob and Esau, into the world after twenty years of marriage. Isaac was sixty years of age at the time they were born (Genesis 25:26). Rebekah had a difficult pregnancy, and when she asked God why, He told her that the twins were fighting in her womb and would continue to do so all of their lives, saying, "Two nations are in your womb, / and two peoples from within you will be separated; / one people will be stronger than the other, / and the older will serve the younger" (Genesis 25:23).

The brothers certainly had different personalities: Esau was outdoorsy and a hunter, while Jacob felt most comfortable in the tents of the family camp (Genesis 25:27). It was a contrast that looked like Cabela's versus Williams Sonoma! We're told that Isaac loved Esau and Rebekah loved Jacob (Genesis 25:28). I know *a lot* of siblings who argue about who is their mom or dad's favorite. My sister, Allyson, and I never had that disagreement—we both knew that I am the favorite! (Just kidding, Allyson.)

Esau, the older twin, sold his birthright to Jacob for stew (Genesis 25:29-34). This is significant because, in that culture, birthright was usually reserved for the firstborn male. Later Rebekah and Jacob plotted to steal Esau's blessing as well—another privilege reserved for the firstborn male—and were successful, creating a chasm between the brothers that was never fully repaired.

Afraid that Esau would kill her favored son, Rebekah sent Jacob on foot to her brother Laban's house in Harran (Genesis 27:43), over two hundred miles away (talk about an ultramarathon!). He would never see his mother again.

In Harran, Jacob met his cousin, Rachel, and fell in love immediately. Jacob asked his uncle Laban for her hand in marriage and pledged to work seven years in exchange. After the seven years, Laban tricked Jacob by switching Rachel with her older sister, Leah, and Jacob married Leah by mistake. A week later, Jacob also married Rachel in exchange for an additional seven years of service (Genesis 29:18-30).

Jacob fathered twelve sons and one daughter through his two wives and their servants:

- From his wife, Leah: Reuben, Simeon, Levi, Judah, Issachar, Zebulun, and Dinah (Genesis 35:23)
- From Bilhah, Rachel's servant: Dan and Naphtali (Genesis 35:25)
- From Zilpah, Leah's servant: Gad and Asher (Genesis 35:26)
- From his wife, Rachel: Joseph and Benjamin. (Genesis 35:24)

After Joseph was born (and before the birth of Benjamin), Jacob decided to return home to his parents in Canaan, but not before another act of deception on Jacob's part. On the way, Jacob had an encounter with God, an all-night wrestling match that humbled him and paved the way for reconciliation between Jacob and Esau (Genesis 32:22-32).

This is a lot to take in, I know. No soap opera would concoct such a story line—no one would believe it. YouTube and reality TV are not prepared to base a show on one man and the four women in his life who help build a nation. And in case you are still a little confused, that's okay. We will unpack the crazy story together again in Week 4. What is important now is just to know that this was the chaos in which Joseph and his brothers were raised. Yet God used their imperfections and their weaknesses to weave together the story of God's people, with Joseph as a pivotal player in the narrative.

Joseph was far from perfect, but his life teaches us about integrity, adversity, and how to handle jealousy. One commentator says it this way: "He was loved and hated, favored and abused, tempted and trusted, exalted and abased. Yet at no point in the one-hundred-and-ten-year life of Joseph did he ever seem to get his eyes off God or cease to trust him. Adversity did not harden his character. Prosperity did not ruin him. He was the same in private as in public. He was a truly great man."[1]

As we embark on this journey together and attempt to find common ground with others, we begin with the story of an epic tale of siblings, jealousy, betrayal, deception, pride, God's faithfulness, and how all these things shaped Joseph into a man of humility and integrity.

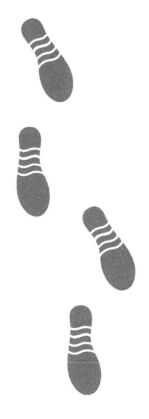

Day 1: That Shade of Green
Is Not Your Color

Today's Key Verses

[3]Now Israel loved Joseph more than any of his other sons, because he had been born to him in his old age; and he made an ornate robe for him. [4]When his brothers saw that their father loved him more than any of them, they hated him and could not speak a kind word to him.

(*Genesis 37:3-4*)

Scripture Focus

Genesis 37:2-4

Joseph seemed to have it all—youthful looks, the favor of his father, and an amazing wardrobe (well, at least one particular item, as we will see). But he lacked one major thing—the respect of his brothers. It looked a little like Kardashian family drama; but instead of hating one another, the brothers only hated Joseph.

When my sister, Allyson, was born, she ruined my life. I had the undivided attention of my parents, the rule of the proverbial roost (well, as much as I could as a four-year-old), and the unencumbered use of all toys and clothes. Her birth meant I now had to share space and attention. And she took WAAAAAAAY more than her share of the attention with all the diaper changes and constant demands for food.

The worst part of her hogging the spotlight happened outside our home. For four years, my curly locks and quick smile won the hearts and eyeballs of every stranger I met. Women would stop my mom on the street to remark about my beautiful hair, and I would bask in the glory. I sang for anyone who would listen and, to the best of my recollection, everyone listened. I became accustomed to the barrage of compliments and accolades.

When Allyson came into the picture, I felt totally eclipsed by her. Friends, family, neighbors, and strangers all stopped to fuss and make silly noises and crazy faces at the new addition to our family. If I was lucky, I *might* get a pat on my head. But there was no denying the truth: There was a new, cuter sheriff in town, and I had been demoted to deputy.

Where do you fall in the birth order of your family?

Did you ever get jealous of a sibling (or another family member)? If so, what happened?

Since the beginning of time (literally), as long as younger siblings have existed, older siblings have complained about the unfair treatment given to the "baby of the family." This was especially true in the case of the sons in the house of Jacob.

Read Genesis 37:2-4.

How did Jacob feel about Joseph? Why?

What did Jacob do that probably caused disharmony among the brothers?

What did Joseph do to make the situation worse?

Draw a picture of what you think the coat might have looked like.

Jacob favored one wife over the other, and his behavior carried on with his sons. He loved Rachel more than Leah; and Rachel's son, Joseph, who was the next-to-youngest, was not just the apple of his father's eye but the whole orchard, at least to his brothers! Strike one against Joseph.

At the beginning of Genesis 37, we learn some background information about Joseph. Verse 2 reminds us of his youth (Genesis 37:2). Youth in itself is not a negative attribute, but it often means a lack of experience, and this was certainly true of Joseph. His lack of experience in working well with others (a lack of emotional intelligence, EQ) did not bode well with his older brothers.

Did you ever tattle on someone? How did that turn out?

What's the difference between tattling and warning someone out of concern?

Tattling is a silly word for an anything-but-silly concept. Tattling involves telling the secrets of others. Rarely does one practice healthy confrontation or redirection when tattling. It's not the same as the biblical accountability we read about in Matthew 18:15-19, where we're encouraged to lovingly confront others who have done wrong and, if they will not listen to us, to take a few witnesses with us for a second conversation. These verses in Matthew tackle the steps we should take as believers when we are in a spiritual "rumble" of sorts and need practical steps to handle the conflict.

According to Matthew 18:15-19, how should we handle those with whom we do not agree?

Tattling, on the other hand, is blabbing to someone else *first*—usually one in authority.

When I was a teacher, I felt it was important to differentiate between "tattling" and "reporting." Reporting involves letting someone know if someone is in danger, if he or she is hurt, or if there is bullying present. Reporting is a vitally important part of safety in the classroom and beyond.

Tattling, on the other hand, is usually designed to avoid healthy confrontation in our everyday relationships. (Picture someone at work who tattles to the boss.) Instead of confronting someone for bad behavior, tattling relies upon a stronger force (usually a parent or teacher) to do the confrontation. Most of the time, people tattle to avoid the discomfort of direct confrontation—and perhaps to get someone else in trouble.

Verse 2 tells us that baby Joseph had a habit of squealing on his older brothers. And even the worst of brothers knows the rule—you don't tattle on one another. Strike two against Joseph.

Everyone knew that Jacob favored Joseph—even Joseph. The ornate coat (of many colors, see KJV) that Jacob bestowed upon him was just one more example of favoritism for all to see. Strike three against Joseph.

No doubt Joseph's coat was his favorite item of clothing. What is your favorite outfit or piece of clothing? Where did you get it?

Is it your favorite because it has a backstory? If so, what is the story?

Now, time to be honest. Have you ever been jealous of someone else's wardrobe or style? If so, where did that jealousy come from?

Probably made of patches of vibrant cloth, the coat reached the wrists and ankles and was a mark of distinction.[2] Many Bible scholars believe that such a token was a dramatic way to illustrate that Joseph, not the eldest son, Reuben, would receive the birthright.[3] As we learned in the Biblical Background for this week, birthright was typically reserved for the first born male—certainly not the much-younger of the clan. So it seems that Jacob, who had stolen his older brother's birthright, may have been planning to buck tradition once again.

Can you think of a time when someone else got the praise or credit you should have received? If so, what was that experience like?

Young Joseph was a shepherd. Jacob was a wealthy man, and his land sheltered many sheep and other livestock. Joseph had learned about shepherding from an early age, and his skills included both the provision (feeding and care) and the protection of the flock, even at the young age of seventeen.

In ancient times, the youngest son often became the shepherd. All the sons would learn the trade (as they were the youngest at some point), but with each male addition to the family, a new future shepherd was born. Although the other siblings may have shared some of the responsibility, the youngest would have shouldered the majority of that responsibility.[4] You might remember another famous shepherd, David. When David was anointed king, Samuel asked Jesse to bring David in from the fields where he was keeping the sheep (1 Samuel 16:11).

Let's put the pieces together. Jacob favored Joseph as the firstborn to his beloved wife, Rachel. To make matters worse, Jacob gave Joseph a special coat to show his favor. Then, Joseph tattled on his brothers when they didn't do their share of the shepherding work.

Jacob put Joseph in a very precarious position. He gave Joseph the coat to communicate his authority over his brothers but did not give him any authority to address issues his brothers might be having in their shepherding responsibilities. He asked Joseph to be the watchdog but removed his teeth by asking him to tattle rather than tackle the issues. Jacob exacerbated the growing mistrust and dislike for his younger son by his brothers.

But as we know, Jacob was used to discord with a sibling. From his birth, he and his brother, Esau, were at odds. Perhaps he did not realize the damage he was doing to the fabric of his family with his favoritism and his delegation of tasks. In any case, it was not kumbaya in the house of Jacob.

Have you ever had jealousy for a sibling (brother or sister) in Christ?

What does jealousy look like? What are the attributes of a jealous person?

When do you find yourself struggling with jealousy? Of whom are you jealous?

So, what's the cure for jealousy? For Joseph's brothers, it meant drastic action. More about that tomorrow. But for now, how can *we* counter jealousy?

We have all felt the pangs of jealousy when we see the positions, plaudits, and possessions of others. We have all wished to "switch places" with others, even for a day. But when we do that, we are not relishing in the life God has given us or rejoicing in the things He has provided for us; and in our ingratitude, we are forgetting just how blessed we are.

Joseph's brothers had much to be thankful for, and they chose jealousy and discontent over thankfulness. They failed to find common ground with Joseph and rejoice in the provision of God. Let's not be like them. Instead, let us shift our gaze from others to God and focus on our blessings!

Call to Action

Choose one or more of the following:

- Write an email, blog, or social media post about the awesomeness of another person.
- Create a "holiday" to celebrate someone in your life, shining the spotlight on someone else. Put the date on the calendar and encourage other people to celebrate this person with you on that day.
- Text someone toward whom you are jealous just to tell them something you appreciate about him or her.
- Leave a big tip for a server, give airline points to someone, or find another way to bless someone. Generosity is a great way to foster a generous spirit toward others, which helps to circumvent jealousy.
- Make a list of people you are jealous of and pray for each by name.

Day 2: Strength in Numbers

Scripture Focus

Genesis 37:5-28

Today's Key Verses

¹⁹*"Here comes that dreamer!" they said to each other.* ²⁰*"Come now, let's kill him and throw him into one of these cisterns and say that a ferocious animal devoured him. Then we'll see what comes of his dreams."*

(Genesis 37:19-20)

One way that sibling rivalry reared its ugly head in my relationship with my sister, Allyson, was in the "sharing" of clothes—and by sharing, I mean that I wore a larger size and could not wear her clothes but she borrowed her "share" of clothes from my closet! It was bad enough that Allyson often borrowed clothes when we were in high school, but she had the audacity to look better in them. It made me want to poke her in the neck. Have you ever felt that way?

Yesterday, we saw the damage that can occur when human beings play favorites. But Joseph wasn't just favored by Jacob; it's clear he also had the favor of God (as we all do, by the way). Yet neither Joseph nor his brothers handled it well.

Read Genesis 37:5-11.

What was Joseph's first dream about?

How did Joseph's brothers respond?

What was Joseph's second dream about?

Did the brothers like this dream any better than the first one? Explain.

How did Jacob respond?

Joseph was also a dreamer. God communicated to him in his dreams, and then Joseph communicated those dreams to his already-envious brothers. The dreams foretold Joseph's rise to leadership, where his brothers would bow to him in submission. I am not a psychology expert, but I think that sharing such tidbits with one's siblings could *never* improve strained relationships. Even Jacob told Joseph he'd crossed a line.

I think I would have sold my sister to the neighbors if she had claimed that God told her that she would be my boss someday. I guess, in a way, that is exactly what Joseph's brothers did to him.

Read Genesis 37:12-28.

What did Jacob ask Joseph to do? Do you think this was a wise decision on Jacob's part? Explain.

How did the brothers respond when they saw Joseph from a distance?

What was the brothers' initial plan?

Who changed their plan? Why?

How did Joseph end up in the hands of the Midianite merchants?

There were enough brothers to have their own five-on-five basketball team with water boys, a baseball team with a few batboys, and a regulation soccer team. They were not in the business of sports, however; they were in the business of jealousy.

Joseph was searching for his brothers and the flocks. He even had to ask a stranger where they might be. Maybe the grass was better at the new location, or maybe the brothers spitefully chose not to tell Joseph where to find them. Either way, he was looking for them.

The Bible tells us, "But they saw him in the distance…" (v. 18). This simple phrase tells us a whole lot about jealousy.

I think one of the roots of jealousy is disconnection. It is easy to make rash judgments and take potshots at people when we do not create the opportunities to get to know them, or when they are far away relationally or geographically. Distance distorts vision. Even for those of us with 20/20 acuity, the farther an object is away from us, the harder it is to see the object clearly. The same thing is true in relationships. We can judge others inaccurately when we have not taken the time to really know them—their hurts, their disappointments, their stories.

The fact that the sentence starts with "but they" is the first harbinger of things to come. These two words tell us that Joseph and his brothers were in different "camps." It also communicates a unity in thought and a ripe environment for groupthink. Such us-against-them mentality can exacerbate an already difficult situation, which is the case with Joseph and his brothers. There is an old adage that says, "There is strength in numbers." I agree with this sage insight, but in the case of Joseph's brothers, there also was weakness in numbers. Their mob mentality moved them from jealousy to violence. The next verse (Genesis 38:19) unfolds their plans to do him harm. I wonder, would any of the brothers have mistreated Joseph if they had encountered him one-on-one?

Have you ever been bullied? If so, write down your memories of that experience.

Have you ever been a bully? If so, can you recall why you acted out?

Do you recall a groupthink mentality in your bullying memories?

I was bullied as a ten-year-old by some of the eighth-grade girls at my school. They were a formidable pack of big hair, loud voices, and popularity. They would hurl rocks and insults at me as I walked down the alley to my home. I was a decent athlete and had competed against some of my aggressors in various arenas, but I never understood their venom against me.

At night, I would dream of flying away from the mean girls. I would re-create the abuse in the alley, but I would fly away from the rocks and unkind words. I have heard that it's common for us to dream we can fly; but sadly, I was not very good at flying. In my dreams, as soon as I was about one hundred feet in the air, my flying abilities became falling abilities. I am sure psychologists would have a field day with the fact that, even in my dreams, I could not seem to "rise above" the bullying.

When I confronted each of the girls separately, each one was remorseful and apologetic. Some were downright nice. But when I saw them with their friends once again, they returned to taunting and harassing me, without skipping a beat.

Often, instances of strong-arming, bullying, and intimidation take place when people feel like they are in a group that agrees with them. Rarely do we see "lone wolf" bullies. We feel empowered and emboldened by the support of others, and their presence often fuels our anger, dissatisfaction, and offense.

"'Here comes that dreamer!'
they said to each other."
(Genesis 37:19)

Reread Genesis 37:19 in the margin. What nickname did the brothers give to Joseph? Do you think it was a term of affection? Explain.

I can hear the sarcasm dripping from the lips of the brothers. I admire when others can use sarcasm effectively and in jest, but this reads more like "SCAR-casm" to me—when people use sarcasm to injure another with their words.

Joseph's brothers mocked him for being a dreamer. They had reasons for responding this way—maybe not good reasons, but reasons nonetheless. Perhaps they were jealous of Joseph's connection to God. Or perhaps they were responding to his lack of humility when telling his brothers about the dreams. Sometimes, we are jealous of the gifts God has given other people. I know I can be. I can see the accomplishments, platforms, and possessions of others and find myself dissatisfied and jealous. In any case, the brothers were clearly salty about Joseph's abilities, because after they plotted to kill Joseph, they said in jest, "Then we'll see what comes of his dreams" (v. 20).

Again, the passage gives hints of groupthink with words such as "us" and "we." Not only did they find strength in numbers, but that seems to have added fuel to the fire of hatred of their brother.

Extra Insight

Anthropologists have found that children from polygamous marriages, such as Jacob's offspring, are more apt to have sibling rivalries.[5] However, this does not excuse the behavior of Joseph's brothers.

Read Genesis 37:21-22. What is different about these two verses?

What do we learn about Reuben?

The first mention of individual thought comes when Reuben, the eldest brother, tried to thwart their plot and suggested that they only throw him in the cistern, but not bring him any harm. His plan was always to return Joseph to his father.

But when Joseph came to his brothers in verse 23, the collective thought returned and the brothers stripped Joseph of his robe and threw him into the empty cistern.

The next reference to an individual comes in verse 26, with Judah, the fourth-born son of Jacob. He offered a plan to sell the dreamer to passing Ishmaelites instead of taking his life. He even threw in the reminder that they were "flesh and blood," after all (v. 27). And sell him, they did.

If the brothers had had the intestinal fortitude to approach Joseph and counsel him (they were his older brothers, after all), level with him about how his behavior had been divisive, or spend time with him, I think the landscape might have looked a lot different.

Write an instance of how the peer pressure of others moved you to do something that was unkind or unhealthy.

What peer pressures do you feel from social media? friends? society? What do you do to combat peer pressure?

What groups do you belong to? (community groups, church groups, teams, or others)

What are you able to accomplish in these groups?

Write about an instance of how the strength of others helped you accomplish something you thought impossible.

Years after I left grade school, one of the bullies from that mean pack of girls recognized me at a clothing store at a local mall. When I first saw her, I pretended not to see her. Although I avoided eye contact with her like the topic of politics at the Thanksgiving table, I felt the heat of her stare for a moment, and then she was standing right next to me. If I had been more athletic, I would have run away like a turkey in November, but instead I just stared at the clothing rack I was standing in front of as if it held the secrets of the universe.

After a quick hello, she introduced herself and asked if I remembered her. Remember her? My therapist remembers her! It took everything in me to refrain from a sarcastic retort that I had a voodoo doll made in her image. Instead, I gently admitted that I remembered who she was.

"We were so jealous of you," she said. "You were the new girl in school and everyone kept saying how great you were. You were tall and confident" (well, I *was* tall), "and it was more than our insecurities could handle. Will you forgive me for my part in all that? Can I buy you lunch?"

Nothing says forgiveness like some Chick-fil-A at the mall.

We had a great time reminiscing about teachers and schoolmates. We shared chicken nuggets, sweet tea, and memories. I had the opportunity to share that I was jealous of them. They were older, cooler, and they had one another.

The meeting was an unexpected blessing for both of us. I have not seen her since, but that day brought a lot of clarity for me—and the opportunity to forgive.

Joseph's brothers had reason to be a bit jealous, but that does not justify their unkind behavior toward their younger brother. Sometimes in our jealousy toward others we forger a critical part of the word *jealousy*—LOUSY. Sometimes our attitudes, behaviors, thoughts, and interactions with others *are* LOUSY with unkindness, bias, and unfairness. If we are to find common ground even with those who seem to have more than we do, we must put our pride aside and extend forgiveness and candor.

Call to Action

Choose one or more of the following:

- Write an article for your church newsletter or website about showing kindness to others.
- Think of someone in your life who may feel put down or misunderstood by others. On small pieces of paper (about fifty to one hundred), write attributes that are special about this person, jot down encouraging Scriptures, and write words of affirmation. Put the papers in a box and give it to the person, telling him or her to pull out a note anytime he or she gets lonely or needs an encouraging word.
- Keep an extra umbrella in your car or at work so you can loan one to someone when it rains.
- Call someone you love, tell this person you love her or him, and share a few things you appreciate most about this person.
- Pray that God would heighten your awareness of anyone if your life whom you are discouraging with your words, attitudes, or jealousy.

Day 3: Coffee Break

Today's Key Verses

[20]*While Joseph was there in the prison, [21]the Lord was with him; he showed him kindness and granted him favor in the eyes of the prison warden. [22]So the warden put Joseph in charge of all those held in the prison, and he was made responsible for all that was done there.*

(Genesis 39:20b-22)

As I write this, I am drinking coffee. For the record, I am always drinking coffee. I love it and it loves me. But once in a while, an overzealous barista or Keurig makes my coffee too hot. Because I have the patience of a circus flea, I drink without testing it first. I hate waiting. Have you ever burned your tongue because you were too impatient to wait for your meal to cool? Me too. Like a million times.

The scalding coffee burns my tongue, and for the rest of that day, the roof of my mouth and temporarily nonfunctioning taste buds remind me that I am impatient. I am reminded of the java malfunction all day.

When my sister was a manager at Starbucks, I asked her how to order my hot beverages. I thought, if I can just order the drinks at a temperature I can immediately drink, without the pain of waiting, my life would be truly perfect. Okay, not really, but I could start with not burning my tongue.

She instructed me to order it at 140 degrees. It sounded so impressive when I would order. I thought I was like one of those schnazzy, sophisticated women whose shoes always match her earrings, belt, and purse. I was a big deal. I never burned my tongue and I felt somehow more awesome than the other plebeian Starbucks orderers who did not know about the secret ability to order drinks the way I did.

One day, when I was feeling especially sassy about my ordering prowess, the barista burst my prideful bubble: "You do know that 140 degrees is just a few degrees higher than the kids' hot chocolate, right?" Busted.

I still order my drinks that way, but these days, I just whisper it to the one taking my order. I'm impatient even with my coffee. I need to take a cue from Joseph, who was patient about a circumstance much more important than a morning cup of java.

Read Genesis 39:1-6a and put yourself in Joseph's sandals.
Think about how much his life had been turned upside down.
In the space on the following page, write about the events

Scripture Focus

Genesis 39:1-23

in these verses as if you were Joseph. Use first person (I, my, mine) to tell the story.

The plot thickens.

After Joseph's brothers sold him to the Ishmaelites, he was placed in the home of Potiphar, the captain of Pharaoh's guard and one of his officials.

Joseph had to wait for God's plan to unfold. Recovering from the shock of being disrobed, thrown into a cistern, and sold into slavery was a lot for anyone to handle, but then he was sold and forced to serve in the house of Potiphar. It was a new culture, language, and social hierarchy for Joseph, and a major contrast from the house in which he had grown up.

Reread Genesis 39:2 to find out how Joseph overcame his circumstances.

God was with Joseph. Despite the injustice and disorientation, God's presence was with Joseph. Many people claim that God is with us in the blessings, but few people will claim with the same ardor that He is also with us in the dark nights.

We do not know how long Joseph served in the house of Potiphar before he won the attention, respect, and trust of Potiphar, but the Bible does tell us that through it all, God was with him and blessed him. God's presence was so obvious to Potiphar, an Egyptian who did not follow the God of Israel, that he gave Joseph charge of his household and everything he owned (v. 4).

Potiphar's delegation paid off. Verse 5 tells us that "the Lord blessed the household of the Egyptian because of Joseph. The blessing of the Lord was on everything Potiphar had, both in the house and in the field."

But this is when the story turns and sounds less like a Sunday school story and more like a daytime Emmy Award–winning soap opera.

Read Genesis 39:6b-20. In the space below, summarize what happened to Joseph.

Potiphar's wife noticed that Joseph was easy on the eyes; verse 6 says that he was "well-built and handsome." When the Bible makes mention of someone's outward appearance, it usually means there is something extraordinary about it; so Joseph must have looked like all the Hemsworth brothers combined (not the commentary of any biblical scholars except this author).

When Joseph refused her advances, in order to honor God and his master, she was humiliated and falsely accused Joseph to her husband. So, Potiphar had Joseph thrown into the prison of Pharaoh (v. 20).

Have you ever been falsely accused? If so, describe it briefly:

Have you ever been lumped into a category before someone got to know you? If so, write about it briefly:

Check your heart. Are there "people groups" you know little about? If so, what preconceived notions do you have about that people group?

How have you been conditioned to be prejudiced or biased against people who are different from you? from your culture?

I have been called judgmental, small-minded, stupid, simple, tone deaf, unkind, unloving, and out of touch because I put "Christian" as my religious views on Facebook. People have made assumptions about my political views, child-rearing practices, and past because I love Jesus.

Even some people in the body of Christ have accused me of things without really knowing all that God has done in my life. I have been accused of not knowing the Scriptures because I am a woman who preaches periodically. I have been accused of being a bad mom because I travel often to speak to others about Jesus. I have been falsely accused of taking sides on some subjects because I have friends who are on all the sides.

When people make unkind, sweeping judgments about me, it is especially hurtful because I did nothing to deserve it. Somehow, it feels like an injustice-and-unkindness sandwich that someone else made and I have to ingest.

Making such judgments about others undermines peace and connection and draws a line in the sand where there need not be one. False assumptions can erode relationships and undermine peace. They cannot burn your tongue, but they can leave a bad taste in your mouth for years to come.

Joseph understood the feeling of false accusation and disconnection. He said no to Potiphar's wife out of love for God and respect for Potiphar. Yet the knowledge that he did nothing wrong may or may not have consoled Joseph when Potiphar had him thrown in prison wrongfully. But God's presence did.

Read the verses below and circle the places where the Lord is mentioned (directly or indirectly):

²⁰**But while Joseph was there in the prison,** ²¹**the Lord was with him; he showed him kindness and granted him favor in the eyes of the prison warden.** ²²**So the warden put Joseph in charge of all those held in the prison, and he was made responsible for all that was done there.** ²³**The warden paid no attention to anything under Joseph's care, because the Lord was with Joseph and gave him success in whatever he did.**

(Genesis 39:20b-23)

God was with Joseph in prison, and once again Joseph was put in charge of things and was a good steward of the opportunity.

Are you in a season of needing to be reminded that God is with you? Explain.

Can you recall a time when you felt God's presence in a strong way?

When you can't feel God's presence, what verses help you remember that God is with you always?

According to biblegateway.com, there are over two hundred instances of God saying "I am with you" to His people.[6] When we realize that God chooses to be with us and never leaves us, even when are not following His Word, we can be encouraged. When we realize that He chooses to be with us when we are feeling crushed by circumstances or choices, we can find hope. And when we share that hope with others, we can find common ground.

Call to Action

Choose one or more of the following:

- Post an encouraging Bible verse or quotation about relationships, or both, on social media.
- Give compliments whenever you can. Ask the Lord to heighten your awareness about who needs a kind word.
- If you are a business owner or leader, leverage your business to do good work and encourage others in your business to be kind and serve others.
- Allow someone to serve you by helping and permit him or her to enjoy the process!
- Pray that God would show you reminders of His presence in various forms.

Day 4: Dream Job

Today's Key Verses

[15]Pharaoh said to Joseph, "I had a dream, and no one can interpret it. But I have heard it said of you that when you hear a dream you can interpret it."

[16]"I cannot do it," Joseph replied to Pharaoh, "but God will give Pharaoh the answer he desires."

(Genesis 41:15-16)

Scripture Focus

Genesis 40:1-23; 41:1-45

The summer before I started high school, my nights were plagued with a horrifying, recurring dream: I was too short to reach the registration table at the high school. I was the size of a mouse (which is hilarious, because I was nearly six feet tall at the time). And despite my best efforts, loudest cries, and vigorous movements (and I had watched *Solid Gold* as a child, so I know vigorous movement!), no one took notice. Students were selecting classes and making friends while I was living out an episode of *Honey, I Shrunk the Freshman*. I would wake up sweating and panting, totally panicked from my dream.

It does not take a clinical psychologist to figure out that I was stressed about being in a new school and finding my place there. My dreams were a manifestation of those insecurities, and although they seem silly now, they ruined endless nights of sleep when I was fourteen.

Joseph not only was a dreamer, but with God's help, he also became a dream specialist. We will be covering a lot of verses today, so hang on!

Read Genesis 40:1-23. In the chart below, record who had the dream, what the dream was about, and what the dream meant according to Joseph.

The Dreamer	The Dream	The Dream's Meaning

When we meet Joseph in Genesis 40, we see that he had gone from Potiphar's prisoner to project manager in the prison. And while there, Joseph used his God-given ability to interpret others' dreams. Then comes perhaps the saddest verse in this story: "The chief cupbearer, however, did not remember Joseph; he forgot him" (Genesis 40:23).

Put yourself in Joseph's sandals again. How would you have felt at this point?

Have you ever helped someone, only to be left out of being recognized? If so, what happened?

Thankfully, Joseph's story doesn't end with being forgotten—although Joseph probably thought nobody remembered him.

Read Genesis 41:1-40.

How long did Joseph remain in prison after the chief cupbearer had been released?

Where did Pharaoh turn first for help, and what led him to summon Joseph?

When Pharaoh asked Joseph to interpret his dreams, what did Joseph say? (v. 16)

Based on this verse, how would you describe Joseph's character? Explain.

Record the two dreams Pharaoh had below:

Dream 1 (vv. 17-21):

Dream 2 (vv. 22-24):

Pharaoh was plagued by bad dreams himself. To be honest, I think my dream was scarier, but whatever.

The sleep of the most powerful man in Egypt was being interrupted by cows and grain. Despite all the magicians, wise men, and leaders Pharaoh consulted, no one seemed to be able to help him make sense of it all—until Joseph was summoned.

Don't miss what Joseph says twice to Pharaoh.

Reread Genesis 41:25 and 28. In your own words, write below what Joseph wanted to be sure Pharaoh understood.

Joseph told Pharaoh that God was revealing what he was going to do. In other words, God was the source of the wisdom. The country was in for a huge famine, and God was warning the leader through dreams in plenty of time to prepare for it.

Joseph interpreted the dreams, warning Pharaoh of seven years of plenty followed by seven years of famine. He even communicated a job description for a wise vizier, which was a leader to help oversee the gleaning and storage of crops to save the lives of Egyptians during the famine years. He also communicated that God would do it soon, thus the reason Pharaoh was given the message in two different dreams, so as not to miss it.

I love that Joseph continued to point Pharaoh to God's abilities instead of his own. Maybe he learned humility inside the cistern, or in the house of Potiphar as a slave, or in prison, or in God's presence in his darkest days, or in the two years until the time the chief cupbearer told Pharaoh about him. But wherever the lesson was learned, it was clear that Joseph had grown in humility.

Bible commentator David Guzik says it this way: "Joseph seems much wiser and perhaps humbler than he was before. If it was true that in the past he told his brothers his previous dreams in a self-glorying way, any such self-confidence was now gone. Joseph knew that God alone had the answer. God's work of character building was being accomplished in Joseph, even when he perhaps thought nothing was happening."[7]

When you think of humility, who comes to mind? Write his or her name below.

What are attributes of people you consider humble? How does one communicate humility in action?

If someone was to ask your closest friends and family to describe you, do you think they would use the word *humble*? Why or why not?

How does one grow in humility?

What can we learn about humility from Joseph's example in Genesis 41?

What happens next can only be described as a shockingly beautiful turn of events.

Read Genesis 41:41-45. List the things that Pharaoh gave to Joseph.

Perhaps it was Joseph's humility that sealed the deal for Pharaoh. None of his officials had the wisdom or blessing from God like Joseph did, and Joseph outlined the responsibilities of the vizier without assuming he should be the man for the job. But Pharaoh gave him the job, his signet ring for his finger, fine robes for his back, a gold chain for his neck, and responsibilities for his shoulders. He also gave him a bride for his heart.

From his marriage to Asenath, daughter of Potiphera (anyone else find it ironic that Potiphera sounds a lot like Potiphar?), two sons are produced. Verse 51 tells us that Joseph got to name them, and he called the first Manasseh, which means "forgetfulness,"[8] because "God has made me forget all my trouble and all my father's household" (v. 51). Joseph was living the dream (pun intended), but he had also endured loss and pain in his years in Egypt, so "to forget" the past seems fitting. To walk in freedom from the past, Joseph needed to forget the wrong done him and to forgive.

Joseph named his second son Ephraim, which means "fruitfulness,"[9] because "God has made me fruitful in the land of my suffering" (v. 52). The name E*phraim* can also sound like the Hebrew for "twice fruitful."[10] By the grace of God, Joseph became "fruitful" in the very land where he had served as a slave and prisoner.

I was named after a character in a book (with some alterations by my mom). My sister, Allyson, was named after June Allyson, American stage, film, and television actress. I know lots of ladies named Patty because they were born on St. Patrick's Day and others named Holly because they were born around Christmas. When my husband and I named our kids, we were a little obsessed about the meaning of their names because of our years of infertility. We wanted their names to be not only a moniker but also a testimony to the goodness of God. Judah, our daughter, was named so because it means "praise," and Leah proclaimed with the birth of her Judah, "I will praise the Lord [for this child]" (Genesis 29:35). Our son Josiah's name means "God has healed." Their becoming part of our family and our lives had undone the years of tears, pain, loss, and heartache, and so we named them accordingly.

Joseph had much about which to be bitter. He had been sold into slavery, falsely accused, wrongly imprisoned, and forgotten. But God had not forgotten Joseph. God's presence was a constant companion in the midst of Joseph's pain, and he wanted the names of his sons to reflect his journey with God. He wanted to communicate, if only to himself, that the damage was undone by the joyful additions of these two boys to his clan.

Humility and forgiveness are competitors for the starring roles in Joseph's life at this time. If we want to love others well and find common ground with those with whom we do not agree, we need to learn from the example of our brother Joseph.

Call to Action

Choose one or more of the following:

- Seek out a seminar or sermon series that pertains to peace and finding common ground with others.
- Encourage others in a practical way. When you open your email each day, write a quick encouraging note to someone.
- Listen to others without interrupting. People don't always want us to suggest a solution. They just want us to listen. We underestimate how important and comforting it is to be heard and understood.
- When you want to help another person, suggest specific ways you can help, such as, "Could we bring food tonight?" or "Let us babysit the kids tonight so you can have a night off." People are less likely to accept help if the offer is too generic.
- Pray that God would put people in your path you can serve.

Day 5: O Brother, Where Art Thou?

Today's Key Verses

⁴Then Joseph said to his brothers, "Come close to me." When they had done so, he said, "I am your brother Joseph, the one you sold into Egypt! ⁵And now, do not be distressed and do not be angry with yourselves for selling me here, because it was to save lives that God sent me ahead of you.

(Genesis 45:4-5)

Scripture Focus

Genesis 42:1-38; 43:1-34; 44:1-33; 45:1-15

My sister and her friends used to spend hours in the sun. Their bronzed bodies were in stark contrast to my pasty, white form. Covered in baby oil (it was the 1980s), they would spend hours listening to good music in skimpy swimsuits and sunglasses. If I had done likewise, the fire engines in my neighborhood would have been envious of my red color. While others go from light to dark when they tan, I go from eggshell to ecru color—*if* I'm slathering myself with suntan lotion. But I will never forget the feel of the one or two sunburns I got in my childhood. There is a reason they are not called "sun warmings." The overexposed sun *burned*—when I changed clothes, when I got in the shower, even when I thought about moving.

Even though it had been years since Joseph felt the burn of his brothers' scorn, the sting of abandonment when they sold him into slavery, and the pangs of loneliness when he thought of his father, I am confident he must have remembered that season in his life on a regular basis. Probably not on his shoulders or on his nose like a sunburn, but deep in his psyche and heart.

When we pick up the story in Genesis 42, we see that Joseph was living large. He was the governor of the land and in charge of the food he had collected in preparation for the drought. He was married with sons, and he was trusted by his boss and the people of Egypt. He also had the power. He was the gatekeeper of the food in a famine, so technically, he got to choose who lived and who died. He was the real MVP (the **M**anaging **V**izier of the **P**haraoh).

Read Genesis 42:1-13. Summarize the events in these verses.

What do you think Joseph might have been feeling when he saw his brothers?

Now look back at Genesis 37:9-10 in the margin. How did Joseph's dream come true?

⁹Then he had another dream, and he told it to his brothers. "Listen," he said, "I had another dream, and this time the sun and moon and eleven stars were bowing down to me."

¹⁰When he told his father as well as his brothers, his father rebuked him and said, "What is this dream you had? Will your mother and I and your brothers actually come and bow down to the ground before you?"

(Genesis 37:9-10)

Then he [Joseph] remembered his dreams about them.

(Genesis 42:9)

When the taste of deception and betrayal had finally dissipated from his mouth, Joseph saw his brothers. If I were in Joseph's shoes, I am afraid the reunion would have looked a lot like an MMA match—minus the spandex and bad acting.

In Genesis 42:6-8, the dreams that Joseph had as a child finally came true. His brothers bowed before him. They did not recognize him. They could never have guessed that he would have survived, much less have risen to such power in Egypt twenty-plus years later. Yet, God had been faithful to Joseph.

Read Genesis 42:9a in the margin. What do you think Joseph felt when he remembered the dreams from long ago?

Joseph was seventeen years old when he was sold into slavery (Genesis 37:2) and in his thirties when he reunited with his brothers (see Genesis 41:46). That's a long time to wait on a dream to be fulfilled. God always comes through—but rarely when or how we expect.

In the verses and days to follow, Joseph seemed to be playing tricks on his unsuspecting brothers. He seemed to be trying to prove their mettle, wanting to know if they, too, had changed and grown in their humility. He put them through a series of tests (like "double-dog dare," Bible-style). In Genesis 42:15, he threatened to let them rot in prison if they did not return with their youngest brother (and Joseph's full brother), Benjamin (like "kick the can," Bible-style). He retained power over them until their true, repentant nature was clear. He even put them in jail (v. 17) for three days (like "go to your room and think about what you've done," Bible-style).

Why put his brothers in jail for three days? Perhaps Joseph wanted time to plan his strategy for dealing with his brothers. Maybe he wanted them to know their fate if they didn't cooperate with him. Or perhaps Joseph wanted to give his brothers a small taste of what he'd experienced in prison.[11]

I used to think he was getting back at them for their treachery, but in verse 18, Joseph showed his hand a bit by admitting that he was a God-fearing man—what could be seen as an unusual act for an Egyptian leader to talk of his reverence for the God of the Jews. As one commentator explains, pharaohs were considered to be the mediators between the gods (plural) and humans and any future gods, so such a claim from Pharaoh would have been extraordinary.[12]

Maybe it was their three days in prison "talking," but the brothers finally admitted their sin. Overcome with grief and remorse, Reuben, the eldest, spoke up and gave an "I told you so":

> ²¹They said to one another, "Surely we are being punished because of our brother. We saw how distressed he was when he pleaded with us for his life, but we would not listen; that's why this distress has come on us."
>
> ²²Reuben replied, "Didn't I tell you not to sin against the boy? But you wouldn't listen! Now we must give an accounting for his blood." ²³They did not realize that Joseph could understand them, since he was using an interpreter.
>
> (Genesis 42:21-23)

Now, the story continues to unfold through to the end of the Book of Genesis—and it is a wild ride indeed. We don't have time to cover it all, so here are some highlights that lead up to the climax of our story. There will not be a test on these things, but like a good barbecue rub to a rack of ribs, these tidbits add much flavor to our picture of Joseph and his brothers:

- Joseph kept Simeon in Egypt while the brothers returned to Canaan with food and silver hidden in their sacks. (Genesis 42:25-38)
- Jacob sent his sons, including Benjamin, back to Egypt for more grain. (Genesis 43:1-15)
- Joseph hosted a dinner for his brothers, with Benjamin getting the largest portion, without revealing his identity. (Genesis 43:16-34)
- Joseph sent the brothers home but ordered a servant to put Joseph's cup in Benjamin's sack. (Genesis 44:1-2)
- Joseph sent troops to go after his brothers and "arrested" them because Benjamin "stole" Joseph's cup. (Genesis 44:3-13)
- Joseph confronted his brothers about the theft and Judah asked to remain in Egypt as Joseph's slave in place of Benjamin because their father loved Benjamin, his youngest son. (Genesis 44:16-33)

That's where we'll pick up with the story.

Read Genesis 45:1-15.

What elements of Joseph's reunion seem most important to you?

Extra Insight

"The three-day imprisonment provided Joseph with time to plan his strategy, and it impressed the brothers with the importance of cooperating....These three days also gave the brothers a taste of what Joseph had endured for three years. Joseph may have intended that they serve one day's imprisonment for each year he had suffered incarceration."[13]

What does this passage tell you about Joseph's faith in God?

How does this story relate to any relationships in your life?

Reread verse 15. What can this verse teach us about overcoming jealousy and repairing broken relationships?

Joseph admitted who he was to his brothers. Sometimes, we get jealous because we forget who we are in Jesus.

In the space below, write some of the things you are in Christ (such as, forgiven, a child of God, loved).

After much weeping, Joseph admits to the brothers who he truly is. And after much discussion on the providence of God, the brothers admitted their regret.

Verse 15, an often overlooked verse in the sermons I have heard preached on Joseph's story, holds the secret to finding common ground with those with whom we do not agree. If we are going to live at peace and combat jealousy, we need to follow the example of Joseph and his brothers: "And he [Joseph] kissed all his brothers and wept over them. Afterward his brothers talked with him" (v. 15).

Instead of talking *about* him (as they had done before selling him into slavery), the brothers now talked *to* him. Through his tears of forgiveness and joy, Joseph communicated how valuable his brothers were to him.

Oftentimes, we feel jealous when we do not feel valued by others. Although we probably don't readily sell siblings in Christ into slavery, we might gossip about them, slander their name, or harbor bitterness. But when we are committed to unity and reconciliation, we communicate with them—and with all people—in a healthy way.

Joseph not only forgave his brothers, he blessed them. Joseph had every right to be mad at his brothers, but instead, he pointed to the sovereignty of God.

Write Genesis 50:20 in the space below.

Is there someone against whom you are harboring bitterness and need to forgive? If so, write a prayer of confession in the space below.

Why do we hold onto unforgiveness and jealousy, in your opinion?

Write Colossians 3:13 below. Underline your contribution. Circle God's contribution.

In the chapters of Genesis that follow, we get to witness the reunion of Joseph and his father Jacob, the flourishing of his family, the blessing of Joseph's sons, the rewards of a long life for Joseph, and a glimpse that the goodwill between Joseph and his brothers was long-lasting (Genesis 50:24). The entire outcome of a family's survival and prosperity, along with generations to follow, changed forever because of Joseph's faith in God and willingness to forgive. It was a true trajectory-change story.

With each day, we have a choice to walk in freedom and forgiveness. When we keep our eyes on Jesus and follow His best for us, our story can be one of a trajectory-change as well. May we learn from the example of Joseph and his willingness to forgive and have faith.

Call to Action

Choose one or more of the following:

- Write a poem about the importance of forgiveness.
- Take your mind off your own insecurities and troubles by sending cards to sick children who are fighting serious illnesses.
- Point out when people do great things. For example, at restaurants, affirm great service by complimenting your servers and telling their managers. Submit an email to the corporate offices, praising the hard work of a colleague. Write a positive online review of a business you appreciate.
- Carry thank-you notes or five-dollar gift cards with you and hand them out to people who do something spectacular.
- Pray for God to help you recall people against whom you are harboring bitterness. Pray for each of them by name and contemplate a reconciliation plan.

Weekly Wrap-up

In this first week of our study, we met the sons of Jacob (who is later called Israel) and discovered the destructive power of jealousy. While the story is peppered with deception, betrayal, and false accusations, the pervasive theme is jealousy. Joseph's brothers were jealous of him, so much so that they faked his death, lied to their father, sold him into slavery, and allowed their hatred of him to blind them.

When they came to Egypt to get food for their families a second time, Joseph had them put in jail for three days. I've read this part of the story a thousand times before, but as I was digging into these chapters of Genesis, I was struck by the importance of their time in jail.

Did Joseph just want to give them a taste of their own medicine? Maybe. No doubt it gave them time to think through their past choices and regrets. But it occurs to me that the concept of three days is clearly important in the Bible; it appears numerous times throughout the Old and New Testaments. Abraham journeyed for three days to obey God and sacrifice Isaac (Genesis 22:14). Jonah sat in the belly of a great fish for three days (Jonah 1:17). Jesus was in the grave three days before he was raised from the dead. Saul was blind for three days after he met Jesus (Luke 24:46).

Without fail, the three days proved valuable time for reflection. Abraham reflected on the promises of God to make him the father of all nations. Jonah reflected on God's call to go to Ninevah. Jesus's followers reflected on his death and his promises to rise from the dead. Saul reflected on the persecution he had administered and the voice of Jesus he heard on the road to Damascus.

I cannot even stick to a diet for three days, but for these people of God, three days proved to be a significant time of reflection and change.

My husband and I attended a silent retreat one weekend. Although it was only twenty-four hours of silence, it felt like a year and a half. We had to use charades to communicate things like, "Where did you put the toothpaste?" "Wow, it is a beautiful day!" and "You are annoying me right now."

But we both benefited greatly from time away from everyday stressors, the din of activity, and the noise of our lives. We both felt closer to God after the twenty-four-hour silence was over. Why? Because concerted listening to God is a rarity in our world. We read Scripture and took the time to contemplate what we read. We prayed and took more than fourteen seconds to express the cries of our hearts to the Lord. I cannot imagine three *days* of silence, but if that is what it takes to hear from God, sign me up.

Joseph's brothers had the opportunity for three days of disconnecting from their routines in contemplation. It was certainly not their choice (as our silent retreat was), but it was a beautiful backdrop for the story of forgiveness that unfolded.

If we want to find common ground in our relationships and our social media accounts, we must eradicate jealousy. We must take time to reflect on the goodness of God and the high value He has placed on each of us. It may take longer than three days, but we must be willing to take a fearless assessment of the places in our hearts where we might be harboring jealousy against another person. If Joseph could do it, we can too, sister!

Group Session Guide:
WEEK 1

Joseph and His Brothers

Combating Jealousy

> Jealousy hinders healthy relationships, but we can fight against it with gratitude for the many ways God has blessed us.

Welcome/Prayer/Icebreaker (5–10 minutes)

Welcome to Session 1 of *Common Ground: Loving Others Despite Our Differences.* Over the next four weeks, we will discover how to find common ground with others so we can build strong, lasting relationships. We will look at obstacles that can hinder our friendships with others, as well as consider tools we can use to establish and nurture meaningful relationships. This week we've explored the powerful and destructive power of jealousy and how to counter it with graciousness and kindness.

Today we will discuss the truths we learned in the past week's study and deepen our commitment to root out the weeds of jealousy. Take a moment to open with prayer, and then allow each person to introduce herself and to recall a time in childhood when jealousy got the best of her.

Video (about 20 minutes)

Play the video segment for Week 1, filling in the blanks as you watch and making notes about anything that resonates with you or that you want to be sure to remember.

Group Session Guide:
WEEK 1

—Video Notes—

Key Scriptures: Proverbs 14:30; 2 Corinthians 10:5; Philippians 4:8; John 14:26

A *heart at peace gives* _____ *to the body,*

   But envy _____ *the bones.* (*Proverbs* 14:30)

_____: Hold envious thoughts captive.

_____: Focus attention on what God is doing in your life.

_____: Allow the Holy Spirit to remind you of who you are in Christ.

Other Insights:

Group Discussion (20–25 minutes for a 60-minute session; 30–35 minutes for a 90-minute session)

Video Discussion

- Read aloud Proverbs 14:30. When have you realized that envy was "rotting your bones"? When have you experienced the ROTS of envy? Share an experience of one of the following:

Group Session Guide: WEEK 1

Resentful longing
Overwhelming discontent
(envy of the) **T**reasures of others
Separation from community

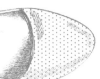

- *How* does envy separate us from community?
- How does envy cloud our judgment of others?
- How does envy take our eyes off of almighty God? How can recapturing our thoughts, refocusing our attention on what God is doing, and reminding ourselves of who we are in Christ help us to overcome envy?

Workbook Discussion

- What does jealousy look like? What are the attributes of a jealous person? (Day 1, page 15)
- What do you think are the roots of jealousy? What triggers jealousy in your life?
- What peer pressures do you feel from social media? friends? society? (Day 2, page 21) What do you do to combat peer pressure?
- How can peer pressure be positive? Talk about a time when the strength of others helped you accomplish something you thought impossible. (Day 2, page 21)
- How have you been conditioned to be prejudiced or biased against people who are different from you? from your culture? (Day 3, page 25)
- Have you ever been treated unfairly because of someone else's bias or prejudice? If so, what was that experience like?
- When you can't feel God's presence, what verses help you remember that God is with you always? (Day 3, page 27)
- What can Genesis 45:15 teach us about overcoming jealousy and repairing broken relationships? (Day 5, page 36)
- How has someone modeled forgiveness for you?

Connection Point (10–15 minutes—90-minute session only)

Divide into groups of two to three and discuss the following:

- How would you describe Joseph's character? (Day 4, page 29)
- Which of Joseph's traits or actions had the most impact on you as you studied his life this week?
- Can you recall a time when something seemed bad, but God used it for good? (Genesis 50:20)

Group Session Guide:
WEEK 1

Closing Prayer (5 minutes)

Close the session by sharing personal prayer requests and praying together. If you like, invite the women to surround those who have shared requests and pray for them aloud. In addition to praying aloud for one another, ask God to help you guard against jealousy in your lives. Ask Him to show you His presence and His goodness, especially in difficult situations and with difficult people.

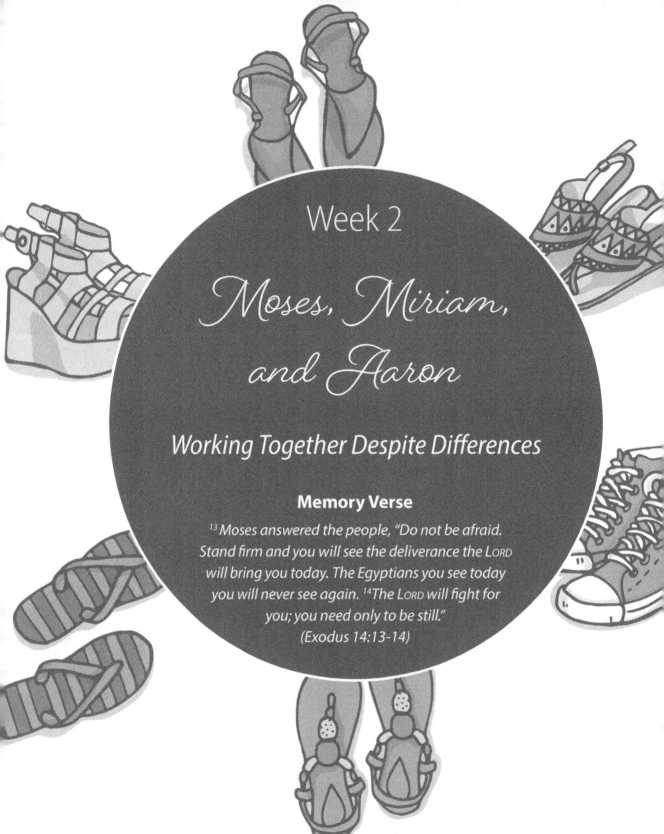

Week 2

Moses, Miriam, and Aaron

Working Together Despite Differences

Memory Verse

¹³ Moses answered the people, "Do not be afraid. Stand firm and you will see the deliverance the LORD will bring you today. The Egyptians you see today you will never see again. ¹⁴The LORD will fight for you; you need only to be still."
(Exodus 14:13-14)

Biblical Background

While the biblical story for Week 1 was contained in a handful of chapters in Genesis, the biblical story of Moses, Aaron, and Miriam spans several books of the Bible and includes many epic stories.

Amram was the father of the three siblings, according to 1 Chronicles 6:1-3. He was of the tribe of Levi, which would become the priestly tribe. Their mother was Jochebed (Numbers 26:57-59).

Miriam was older than Moses. We know this since, when Jochebed placed Moses in the reeds of the Nile in a little "floating ship" made of sticks (Exodus 2:1-4), Miriam "stood at a distance to see what would happen to him" (v. 4). Aaron was older than Moses as well, by three years (Exodus 7:7). That being said, Moses was listed first in Micah 6:4, despite the cultural norm of listing the eldest first.

We also know that Moses was "educated in all the wisdom of the Egyptians" (Acts 7:22). Although Jewish blood coursed through his veins, Egyptian culture and language coursed through his early years. His upbringing was different from that of his siblings, but when they began working together, they acted like most siblings. Some days they got along swimmingly, and other days, they didn't. On one day, one of them even got leprosy because of that person's antics. Oh wait, never mind. We will cover that later.

But just like me and Aqua Net in the 1980s, the three siblings were an incredible team; each one had different gifts and strengths from the Lord. Miriam was a prophetess (Exodus 15:20). Aaron was the high priest of Israel (Exodus 28:1; 38:21; Numbers 3:6; Psalm 99:6). Moses was also a priest (Psalm 99:6) and a prophet for God to the nation of Israel, who had a connection to God unlike any other prophet in the Bible (Deuteronomy 34:10-12). Moses led the nation of Israel out of Egypt and into the land of Canaan; and, although he was a leader, he was the humblest man on Earth (Numbers 12:3). He was also faithful to God, being likened to Christ as an example of a faithful leader (Hebrews 3:5).

But the siblings were not perfect. Aaron doubted and led people into idolatry (Exodus 32:1-6). Miriam was a grumbler. She and Aaron gossiped against their brother (Numbers 12:1-2). Moses did not follow God's specific instructions (Numbers 20:2-13). Oh, and did I mention that Moses turned up on "Pharaoh's Most Wanted" list for killing an Egyptian (Exodus 2:11-12)?

We can learn much from the relationship between Moses, Aaron, and Miriam.

- that God knows us and chooses to use us anyway, placing us in positions for which He has equipped us in order to make a difference;
- that we must fulfill our callings with humility and honor;
- that leadership requires cooperation, with God and with others;
- that we should work in the best interests of others;
- that we should appreciate the contributions of others; and
- that teamwork really can be the key to success.

Day 1: Setting the Stage

Scripture Focus

Exodus 2:1-24

Today's Key Verses

[10]When the child grew older, she took him to Pharaoh's daughter and he became her son. She named him Moses, saying, "I drew him out of the water."

[11]One day, after Moses had grown up, he went out to where his own people were and watched them at their hard labor. He saw an Egyptian beating a Hebrew, one of his own people. [12]Looking this way and that and seeing no one, he killed the Egyptian and hid him in the sand. . . .

[15]When Pharaoh heard of this, he tried to kill Moses, but Moses fled from Pharaoh and went to live in Midian.

(Exodus 2:10-12, 15)

When I first laid eyes on my husband, I thought he was a rotten apple. I had heard rumors that he was overconfident and slightly self-righteous. He was in the elite choir for upperclassmen when I was a freshman, so we had little interaction (if any), but I was certain he was a bad guy. He was kind of handsome (okay, *really* handsome), but I heard that he never gave anyone the time of day, despite many girls who had a crush on him.

But boy, did that man have a voice. Wowza. When he sang, I swear the earth stood still out of reverence until he was done. That rotten apple had mad skills!

A mutual friend introduced us to each other, and one of my roommates encouraged our relationship. She and Scott had been best friends in high school, and she proceeded to give us both secret intel on the other. I quickly figured out that he was not self-righteous; he just wanted to follow Jesus. He paid little attention to crushes because he wanted to finish school on time and earn enough money for grad school. He was focused. Driven. Misunderstood.

The story of Moses, Aaron, and Miriam spans the vast majority of the Book of Exodus. Although most believers have heard 1,487 sermons, Sunday school lessons, flannelgraph illustrations (you know who you are), and VeggieTales episodes on the subject, I think these three have been a bit misunderstood. Many see Moses as a bold leader and his siblings as meek traveling companions, but the truth is that they were three imperfect people pointing others to a perfect God—and a strong team of leaders when they worked together.

Read Exodus 2:1-4.

Which characters are introduced in these four verses?

What did Moses's mother notice about him?

How did Moses's mom protect him?

The beginning of Exodus 2 sounds a little like a condensed and twisted "once upon a time" story. Guy meets girl. Guy marries girl. Guy and girl have three kids, the last of whom is a son. Girl hides son from evil dictator, then puts the child in a basket and puts it among the reeds. Tale as old as time, right? *Wrong*.

Verse 2 says Moses's mom "saw that he was a fine child." Now, that doesn't mean he was immediately in an Egyptian baby contest or that she would have let him die if he were homely.

I was *not* a beautiful baby. I had jet-black hair that stood on end despite constant combing and cajoling from my mother. I surely would not have been called "fine"—no one knocked on our door asking if I would be in their baby food commercials or life insurance ads, but my mom was fine with that. She thought I was beautiful, just as Moses's mom thought her baby boy was too. It's important to note, however, that in ancient times beauty was considered an indication of divine favor.[1] Hebrews 11:23 says, "By faith Moses' parents hid him for three months after he was born, because they saw he was no ordinary child." So the focus should be on Moses's parents' faith, not Moses's looks.

Miriam, Aaron, and Moses (in that order) were born into the tribe of Levi, who was the third son born to Jacob. This tribe would later be set aside as priests who mediated the covenant of God with Israel[2]—we might say they were the "overseers" of the Law. The nation of Israel, although believers in God, were trying to stay off the radar of Pharaoh. The Egyptian leader was afraid that the Hebrews would revolt against him because their population had exploded, so he issued a decree that all male Hebrew babies must be killed.

Aaron had already been born, so he was not in danger, but when Moses entered the scene, something had to be done. His mother defied Pharaoh's edict and hid her son as long as she could. Then she put him in a basket (I envision the "egg" of Baby Yoda in the *Mandalorian* series) and set him among the reeds dotting the edge of the Nile River. Pharaoh's daughter saw the basket, ordered a servant to retrieve it, and when it was all said and done, Moses's mother ended up nursing Moses. Happily ever after, right? *Wrong*.

Read Exodus 2:5-10.

Who found Moses?

How did God intervene in the life of infant Moses?

Scan back over these verses, along with verses 1-4. Who is mentioned by name?

Moses is the only one who is actually named. The beginning of this story sets the stage for the relationship between Moses and his siblings. We will see the importance of that later.

Miriam, Moses's sister, watched out for Moses (v. 4) and then interceded for him (v. 7) when Pharaoh's daughter found him. Those were typical big-sister responsibilities in my house. I was often given the responsibility of looking out for my sister, Allyson, and interceding on her behalf if she needed it. I would walk with her to school, make sure she had what she needed for the day, and often-times sign her permission slips if we had forgotten to have our mom do it. I was not a perfect big sister, but I did my best.

For many years after Moses returned to the palace of the pharaoh, he probably had little or no contact with his siblings, yet God was preparing each of them individually for the work He had in store for them to do together.

Imagine the difference between growing up as a slave oppressed by a heart-less leader and growing up in the palace of that leader. Moses was raised by a daughter of an Egyptian supreme high priest. Verse 10 tells us that Moses became the son of the pharaoh's daughter. Imagine the huge chasm of culture in the areas of faith, traditions, upbringing, privilege, expectations, language, and hope for the future. Despite the menagerie of differences with the siblings, God would ultimately "work all things for good" (Romans 8:28) in their stories.

What was your favorite food as a child? favorite music? How does that reflect your background?

What are three attributes you possess now that you know come from your background/family of origin?

Before we were married, my husband pursued his master's degree on a full-ride scholarship to the University of Southern California. USC is one of the most beautiful campuses in our nation. This idyllic environment has a rich history of education, private research, a strong football program, and a serious rivalry with UCLA. It is located in the city of Los Angeles, but part of its perimeter falls into an area with a history of unrest, gang violence, and crime.

While Scott was at USC and I was still going to school in Arizona, I ventured out to visit him. Although I was overcome with admiration for the surroundings, I was oblivious to the area and its challenges. Scott had a voice lesson, and I offered to wait for him in the quad area. On our way to the campus, I could not help seeing the trash in the car. Scott drove hundreds of miles each week to commute and spent a lot of time in the car—and his backseat told that story. I decided that instead of just waiting, I wanted to take that car and wash it. This was before Google maps, so I just thought I would drive until I found one. And find one I did. I was probably five miles from campus, in a neighborhood with visible economic blight and dilapidated buildings, but I was too busy basking in the beauty and sunshine of a Southern California day to care.

When I located the car wash, I got out of Scott's car and began to wash it. Immediately, a large man stood in front of the car, just far enough away to avoid the blast of the car wash sprayers. At first I paid no attention, but after a few minutes I finally asked, exasperated, "Can I help you?"

"Why are you here?" he asked, clearly perturbed with my presence.

"Because my boyfriend can't seem to keep his car clean, so I thought a car wash might do the trick," I sarcastically retorted.

"No, why are you here?" he asked again, this time with an accent on the last word of the sentence. I wasn't sure what to say next.

"I am sorry, should I not be here?"

"This is not a good neighborhood. Lots of bad things happen around here. YOU DO NOT BELONG HERE. I will wait here until you are done so you stay safe, but you need to be more careful in the future," he scolded me.

And wait he did. He was a wall of a human. His bulging muscles and icy stare made me feel safe and scared at the same time. He shook his head in disgust and let out a disapproving sigh every few minutes. If the US Olympic committee was looking for a competitor for fastest car washer in America, I think I would have qualified that afternoon.

When I finished, I thanked him profusely and got out of that parking lot like there were chili peppers in the gas tank.

Later, when I explained to Scott the location of the car wash, his eyes widened. "Sweetheart, that is not a very safe neighborhood."

"I know that now, but if you are ever in doubt that angels exist, just know that I met one today and he lives in Los Angeles."

I may not have belonged in that neighborhood, but I was only there for twenty minutes. Moses, however, lived every day somewhere he did not belong by birth—in a palace. He learned to dress according to Egyptian customs and speak their language, which was different from that of his biological siblings.

However, because he was taken back to his mother as an infant to nurse until he was weaned, he was exposed to the Hebrew way of life and likely to teachings about a God the Egyptians did not follow. We can only speculate how that affected Moses's decisions later in life, but I cannot help thinking it did.

Less than a dozen verses after Moses is born, the Bible recounts his first criminal offense.

Read Exodus 2:11-14 below and answer the questions that follow.

¹¹*One day, after Moses had grown up, he went out to where his own people were and watched them at their hard labor. He saw an Egyptian beating a Hebrew, one of his own people.* ¹²*Looking this way and that and seeing no one, he killed the Egyptian and hid him in the sand.* ¹³*The next day he went out and saw two Hebrews fighting. He asked the one in the wrong, "Why are you hitting your fellow Hebrew?"* ¹⁴*The man said, "Who made you ruler and judge over us? Are you thinking of killing me as you killed the Egyptian?" Then Moses was afraid and thought, "What I did must have become known."*

(Exodus 2:11-14)

What triggered Moses's anger?

What does this response tell you about Moses?

Describe the emotional quandary Moses might have experienced.

What components of your personality that stem from your upbringing do you wish you could change? Why?

We can deduce a few things from these verses. First, despite living in the palace, both Moses and those who raised him were aware that he was "not one of them." He considered the Hebrews "his own people," which must have meant he was well aware of his disconnection from the throne of Pharaoh. Second, Moses had empathy for his people. When one of them was suffering a beating, he could not stand idly by and allow it, even though he knew it could mean his demise. He killed the Egyptian when he thought no one was looking and hid the body (v. 12).

Although Moses looked around to see if any humans were watching, he failed to account for the fact that Yahweh, the God of the Hebrews, would see his actions. He acted out of his flesh instead of his faith, a struggle he would wrestle with later.

Let's find out the conclusion of this part of Moses's story.

Read Exodus 2:15-24.

Where did Moses end up? Why?

What happened to Moses while he was there?

How do verses 23-25 set the stage for future events in the Book of Exodus?

Pharaoh got word of the murder and, despite the fact that Moses had grown up in his palace, Pharaoh wanted him dead. Moses fled to Midian where he was again sheltered by the family of a priest (Exodus 2:16, 21), but this time, it's possible that the priest worshipped God (as some scholars suggest based on Exodus 18). Moses endeared himself to the family of Reuel, also known as Jethro, by helping his daughters. Eventually, Moses would become a shepherd, a skill that would come in handy when leading thousands of people in later seasons of his life.

Why is it important to know Moses's background? If we want to work in the best interests of others and interact well with them, we must respect those with whom we come into contact. Understanding someone's history and life experiences can go a long way in working with people.

Moses was shaped by his upbringing in the house of Pharaoh; but ultimately, he was sculpted into the man God needed him to be through his experiences, mistakes, and adventures. Likewise, we are shaped by our backgrounds—our ethnic and cultural heritage, traditions, and formative experiences—as well as our later experiences, mistakes, and decisions. Sometimes learning to appreciate and work well with others begins with understanding more clearly their backgrounds, experiences, and perspectives—especially when they are different from our own. Just as Moses, Aaron, and Miriam had to learn to maneuver differences, we can do the same by learning about the cultures, backgrounds, and perspectives of others.

Call to Action

Choose one or more of the following:

- Visit museums in your area and appreciate the artistic abilities of others. Many museums include a description of each artist's background and how it shaped his or her art.
- On special days such as Mother's Day, Father's Day, and Veteran's Day, check in with friends who have lost a loved one. Loss changes us in many ways, and connecting with others in their loss can help us understand them and give us perspective regarding how to connect with them, work with them, and love them.
- Every day, write down three things for which you are grateful and how each one adds value to your life. Do the same thing with three people. Work in the best interests of others by serving them out of gratefulness for their contribution to your life.
- Pray for your brothers and sisters in Christ in your church, your community, and beyond.

Day 2: To Love and Obey

Scripture Focus

Exodus 3:1-15; 4:1-17

Today's Key Verses

[11]*Moses said to God, "Who am I that I should go to Pharaoh and bring the Israelites out of Egypt?"*

[12]*And God said, "I will be with you. And this will be the sign to you that it is I who have sent you: When you have brought the people out of Egypt, you will worship God on this mountain."*

(Exodus 3:11-12)

I am not a fan of magic. My husband and I saw David Copperfield in Las Vegas one year and, although the show was indeed spectacular, I remember thinking, *We just spent a lot of money to have someone fool us.* I don't like feeling like a dolt. I hate to feel tricked, bamboozled, cheated, conned, deceived, duped, hoodwinked, misled, swindled, flimflammed, misinformed, and outwitted. I think we all do. A magic trick is based on an elaborate ruse to divert the eyes and/or attention long enough to trick them—thus the reason it is not called a magic *realism*. Even *illusion*, which sounds more kind to the one who falls for such a thing, is defined this way: "A thing that is or is likely to be wrongly perceived or interpreted by the senses. A deceptive appearance or impression. A false idea or belief."[3]

When Exodus 3 opens, we find Moses about to encounter God in a truly amazing way. It is no magic trick, however.

Read Exodus 3:1-10.

Use the space below to outline the interaction in this passage.

Which verse(s) seem most significant to this story? Why?

Which verse(s) seem most relevant to your story right now? Why?

Unlike David Copperfield and other magicians like him, the goal of the burning bush was not to confuse or confound but to connect. The sight of the face of God would have been too much, so God chose something (a bush) that Moses must have seen a thousand times a day as a shepherd—a bush (well, not a burning one)—and used it to speak to Moses. God used the ordinary and did something extraordinary—both in the shrubbery and in Moses.

God explained that He had heard the cries of His people being oppressed by the Egyptians. Don't miss that. While our focus this week is on the relationship of the three siblings in this story, their story was part of a much larger one—God's deliverance of His people. God heard them and responded. That same God hears your cries—and He will act on your behalf. Not always in the timing or way you want, but He will help you.

What cry of your heart is God hearing these days?

God heard His people and wanted to send Moses as His spokesperson to bring deliverance, but Moses balked.

Read Exodus 3:11-15. Using the prompts below, rewrite this interaction in your own words.

(v. 11) Moses said...

(v. 12) God said...

(v. 13) Moses said...

(vv. 14-15) God said...

How do you think you would have responded to this invitation?

I relate to Moses more than I would like to admit. He was comfortable where he was, uncomfortable about his past, and uncertain about his abilities. He was staring at the miracle of a burning bush (without the bush being consumed) and yet, he could not translate that awesomeness to the idea that God could do mighty things in and through him. His question showed both his insecurities in himself and in the character of God. That is why I love that God met Moses's insecurity with the ultimate security system:

"I will be with you." (v. 12)

If we are going to recognize that God places us in a position to make a difference, we need to remember that He calls us to obedience, not to self-reliance. God knew Moses's inadequacies and strengths. He was privy to Moses's past, cultural background, weaknesses, ability to speak Egyptian, heart for God's people, insecurities, and speech problem.

What do you consider your three greatest weaknesses?

1.

2.

3.

What do you consider your three greatest strengths?

1.

2.

3.

Moses was shaped by his family of origin, his upbringing, and his job as a shepherd. Which of your strengths are a direct result of your background?

Moses allowed his insecurities to speak louder than the security of God's promises, which spills over to Exodus 4.

Read Exodus 4:1-12.

How did God demonstrate patience with Moses in these verses?

How did Moses respond to God's miracles?

After discussion, miracles done with a shepherd's staff and a cloak, detailed plans, promises in great number, and persuasion in great fervor, Moses still was not convinced that God's presence and power could overcome his puniness. And despite the prodding and power of God, Moses refused to obey.

Have you ever failed to obey because you were too busy trying to persuade our all-knowing God that you couldn't do it? I have.

Share my faith with my neighbor, God? I don't know enough Scripture, and it might make things uncomfortable when we see each other on the street. My faith is inadequate.

Support a missionary? Lord, You have seen my bank account. There is no way I can spare $25 a month to make a difference across the world when I cannot even seem to keep my financial act together where I live. My resources are inadequate.

Open my home to kids for foster care? Lord, You have seen my small house and limited schedule. Plus, You know how impatient I can be. My skills are inadequate.

Mentor a teen? Lord, You know what a disaster area I was when I was a teenager. Plus, I am probably too old and too outdated to make a difference. My relevance is inadequate.

Volunteer in kids' ministry? Lord, You know how broken my home was growing up. I am hardly a great example. My past disqualifies me and my present is inadequate.

Have you ever tried to talk God out of doing what He has asked you to do? If so, what happened?

God cut through Moses's excuses and left him with no more excuses:

¹³Moses said, "Pardon your servant, Lord. Please send someone else."

¹⁴Then the Lᴏʀᴅ's anger burned against Moses and he said, "What about your brother, Aaron the Levite? I know he can speak well. He is already on his way to meet you, and he will be glad to see you. ¹⁵You shall speak to him and put words in his mouth; I will help both of you speak and will teach you what to do. ¹⁶He will speak to the people for you, and it will be as if he were your mouth and as if you were God to him. ¹⁷But take this staff in your hand so you can perform the signs with it."

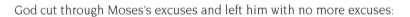

(Exodus 4:13-17)

I have always been insecure in regard to my sister, Allyson. She is smarter, prettier, and stronger than I am. She makes more money, lives in a better house, and frankly, is cooler than I ever will be. She is also wicked good at math. Like Crazy Town good.

Years ago, when we were both still teenagers, Allyson and Dad were having a discussion. She had done poorly on an English assignment, and he was trying to encourage her, albeit not successfully. He said she was good at math while I was good in English. He both reaffirmed my insecurity about my math skills and her insecurity about her writing skills in one fell swoop. I overheard their conversation, and to this day, we both still allow those words to affect us. She is highly successful in her career; but periodically, she will still send me a document for me to check its grammar. She is actually a great communicator, but our dad's words still echo in her brain. I am also pretty good at math. When I taught algebra, no matter how many problems I did right, whenever I made a mistake I would think in my head, "That's okay, Allyson is the one who's good at math."

Moses and Aaron may have had similar issues. Moses knew he wasn't good at speaking, and he knew his brother was. So, Aaron was roped into helping him. And help him he did. He was the mouthpiece for the Lord to the Egyptian leadership, asking them to release the Hebrew slaves. He also helped Moses lead through the plagues (Exodus 7–11), Passover (Exodus 12), and the Ten Commandments (Exodus 20). Later, Aaron was made a priest because of his willingness to serve the Lord (Exodus 28).

> **Moses had Aaron, someone who was strong in an area where he was weak. Name someone in your sphere of influence who has a gift or talent in an area where you are weak. How do you complement each other?**

> **Is God calling you to serve in an area where you are weak and may struggle to trust Him? Explain.**

God placed Moses in a Hebrew home to be born, an Egyptian palace to be raised, and a shepherding community to learn leadership. God gave Moses a family of origin with two siblings, Aaron and Miriam, who could help him on his journey. If we are going to be people who can find common ground, we need to trust that God, not our abilities or training or background, qualifies us to do so.

Call to Action

Choose one or more of the following:

- Going places and doing things outside of your comfort zone can help you develop empathy. Go somewhere or do something outside your comfort zone.
- Ask someone who is overwhelmed—perhaps feeling inadequate, insecure, or weak—if you can pick something up for him or her. New

parents, caregivers for ill family members, and foster parents are great candidates.

- If you overhear gossip about someone (particularly related to her or his abilities), encourage the conversation to stop and direct it in a more positive direction.
- Pray that God would allow you to see the beauty of your background and experiences and how all has shaped you into who you are today.

Day 3: Practically Imperfect in Every Way

Scripture Focus

Numbers 20:1-13;
Exodus 2:1-6, 19-24;
Numbers 12:1-16;
Romans 3:23-24

Today's Key Verses

[23]All have sinned and fall short of the glory of God, [24]and all are justified freely by his grace through the redemption that came by Christ Jesus.

(Romans 3:23-24)

Do you ever get a song in your head and cannot get it to go away? I call such catchy tunes "brain worms" because they worm their way into my brain and never let go. It is rarely a hymn or praise song that falls into this category. Usually, songs that stick in my head are either untimely or inappropriate. I will attempt to hum it away, try and switch to another song altogether (never successfully), or just lean into it in hopes that my brain will finally move on to something else.

One song that pretty consistently gets into my head is a ditty from the great philosopher Miley Cyrus. Okay, maybe not a great philosopher, but a singer who has more than one song that worms its way into my brain.

A portion of the lyrics of her song "Nobody's Perfect" are superglued to my psyche. She's singing about struggling with being imperfect and living and learning, and then she proclaims,

> And if I'm messing up sometimes (hey),
> nobody's perfect.[4]

Okay, so it is no magnum opus, but its charm is undeniable and its appeal vast. The message is the part that sticks with me the most. Nobody's perfect (although some of us would like to give it a shot).

Moses, Aaron, and Miriam experienced some truly epic events. They saw the hand of God in the plagues and the protection of the Lord in the plague of the firstborn during Passover. They witnessed firsthand the parting of the Red Sea, the salvation of their people from the hands of Pharaoh, a myriad of other miracles, and the guiding of God's people through the wilderness. Moses received the Ten Commandments and actually saw God—well, at least His backside.

Exodus 6 spells out just how important they were to giving relief to the Israelites from Egyptian oppression:

> ²⁸Now when the LORD spoke to Moses in Egypt, ²⁹he said to him, "I am the LORD. Tell Pharaoh king of Egypt everything I tell you."
>
> ³⁰But Moses said to the LORD, "Since I speak with faltering lips, why would Pharaoh listen to me?"
>
> (Exodus 6:28-30)

Yet Moses always doubted that he was a sufficient leader and speaker, so God consistently reminded Moses to focus on Him and what He could accomplish through those who are willing. God is so patient with us, isn't He?

The story of Moses and his siblings spans the books of Exodus, Leviticus, Numbers, and Deuteronomy. Their narratives span many chapters in these books, and although they did many things right, they also had their fair share of missteps.

Moses's Leadership

In Numbers 20, we read about a time when Moses showed his fallibility.

Read Numbers 20:1-13.

Summarize the story in your own words.

How did Moses disobey God's instruction?

Why was this one action such a big deal?

What were the consequences of Moses's actions?

There is nothing more obnoxious to me than listening to an adult whine. Often it is a mixture of privilege, pride, and pathetic all in one, and it is terribly unbecoming. I have done my fair share of whining regarding traffic, but I usually reserve it for inner dialogue because, frankly, no one wants to hear it. In their whining, the people were opposing Moses and Aaron and questioning the goodness of God and His plans. They complained about a lack of water (among other things), so Moses and Aaron went before the Lord. The Lord gave Moses explicit instructions about speaking to the rock with his staff in his hand in front of the people so that water would come from it.

This is where Moses messed up. He then asked the Israelites, "Must we bring you water out of this rock?" (v. 10). As if Moses and Aaron had the power to do so without God. It sounds like something that a perturbed parent might say: "Must I pull this car over to address your quarreling?"

Moses did not speak to the rock as God had commanded, but instead he struck it twice. Despite the fact that Moses and Aaron did not follow the instructions exactly, God did make the water gush out of the rock. But there were consequences to their disobedience.

I have a couple of questions. First, why such a harsh penalty for striking a rock? Seriously. These two guys put up with a lot from the Hebrew people, and after one act of disobedience, they don't get to go into the very land they were leading the people to. Sounds harsh to me. Second, why did Aaron get punished when Moses was the one who disobeyed?

The issue wasn't just that Moses used the staff—the issue was trust. Earlier in the journey, God had told Moses to strike a rock (Exodus 17:6), so one commentator suggests Moses didn't trust that just speaking to a rock would work.[5] It seems Moses didn't understand that the rod was a symbol of God's authority, not some magic wand.

In addition to Moses's disbelief, his actions were unholy. He lectured the people (which God hadn't told him to do). His heart was full of anger and contempt. This anger and frustration made God look no different from the temperamental gods around them. Moses did not represent God's love or mercy.[6]

So, what about Aaron? His actions didn't get him in trouble. It was his *inaction*. Aaron had heard what God told Moses, but he didn't intervene when Moses lectured the people. And he didn't stop Moses from hitting the rock the second time. He sat and watched the scenario unfold. Perhaps this is a lesson for all of us about sitting on the sidelines when we see something wrong taking place.

Despite all the signs, wonders, glorious miracles, acts of provision, and love, Moses struggled with trust; and neither he nor Aaron got to see the Promised Land.

The lesson for us: We must not limit God.

Aaron's Leadership

As we have seen, Aaron was not perfect either. God set him apart to be a priest and lead the people, but when things got ugly, he buckled.

Read Exodus 32:1-6. Use the space below to draw a picture of this scene—or the calf. Don't worry about being an artist!

How would you describe Aaron based on these verses?

Talk about giving in to peer pressure! Aaron didn't hesitate to give the people what they wanted. Poor leadership shifts with the winds of popularity. Strong leadership stays the course in the face of compromise and opposition. Unfortunately, Aaron's behavior in this story doesn't get any better.

Read Exodus 32:19-24.

What did Moses witness when he returned to the camp?

What did Moses ask Aaron? Paraphrase the question in your own words.

What was Aaron's excuse? What fanciful story did he tell?

A golden calf just popped out of fire? Really, Aaron? That's the best you can do? Not only did Aaron give in to the whims of the people, but he also failed to take responsibility for his own actions.

I have always struggled with the story of the golden calf. It seems foolish to make a statue out of the gold from one's jewelry collection, watch it being formed, and then worship it as divine. How can a person find solace in something they just created with their own hands? Well, actually, now that I think of it, I have been known to do that with cheesecake.

In all seriousness, we turn to all sorts of pleasures and distractions when we feel anxious, angry, scared, or restless. The idol may not be made of gold, but it's a cheap substitute for the peace and purpose that only God can provide.

Miriam's Leadership

Despite the fact that she led others in music and song (Exodus 15:20-21) and was honored with the title of prophetess (Exodus 15 and Numbers 12), Miriam joined Aaron in speaking against Moses.

> **Read Numbers 12:1-16.**
>
> **Why were Miriam and Aaron complaining? List the two reasons. (vv. 1-2)**
>
> **How did God react to Miriam and Aaron? (vv. 4-10)**
>
> **Why do you think Miriam got leprosy but Aaron didn't?**
>
> **How did Moses respond? (v. 13)**

The fact that Miriam's name was listed first, and given that she was the only one punished, leads some scholars to believe she was the instigator of this gripe session against Moses.[7] The reason? Probably Moses's marriage to a Cushite. It is likely that his first wife, Zipporah, had died, and while the second marriage wasn't prohibited, Miriam may have felt as if her authority and influence had been diminished by this "outsider."[9] She and Aaron also grumbled that God had not only spoken through Moses but also through them.

Another interesting tidbit is that Miriam's name actually means "bitterness." She lived up to her name, along with her brother, in this season.[10] This almost feels like dramatic irony.

These siblings were imperfect indeed. We all are, but God uses us nonetheless. If we want to work well together and learn to live in peace, we must accept one another's imperfections. We need to cut one another slack and recognize our own shortcomings instead of judging those of others.

You and I are not perfect. Romans 3:23-24 reminds us of that truth.

Read Romans 3:23-24. Rewrite these verses in your own words.

What character flaw in other people are you most quick to see? Why?

To which of the three siblings can you most relate: Moses, with his impatience; Aaron, with his inaction; or Miriam, with her insecurity? Explain.

Aaron, Moses, and Miriam—known for being pioneers of leadership of the people of God—were flawed. But God did not stop using them as leaders when they messed up. Instead, God used those flaws to draw each of them closer to Him—and others in the process. In the same way, God knows your flaws and imperfections. They don't surprise Him. He won't put you on the sidelines when you make mistakes. In fact, He can use those mistakes for your good and His glory if you're willing to allow Him to work in your heart.

Call to Action

Choose one or more of the following:

- Listen to others with the intent to understand, not to be understood.
- Moses and Miriam struggled with whining. If you find yourself griping or complaining about someone this week, stop and look for something positive to affirm in the other person.
- If you find yourself judging another this week, remember that Aaron and Miriam did not assume the best about their brother, Moses. They assumed the worst, and in the process, they created division. Give the other person the benefit of the doubt, especially if there is conflict between you.
- Pray that God would use your ministry, mistakes, and missteps to point others to Him.

Day 4: Humility Is Key

Scripture Focus

Ecclesiastes 4:9-12

Today's Key Verses

> ⁹*Two are better than one,*
>   *because they have a good return for their labor:*
> ¹⁰*If either of them falls down,*
>   *one can help the other up.*
>
> (*Ecclesiastes 4:9-10*)

For one summer in my youth, I worked at a local pool as a lifeguard. I wanted a cool way to help others and thought that saving drowning swimmers and being a hero sounded so epic. When I trained to be a lifeguard, I thought it would look a lot like being an actress in the *Baywatch* cast. Instead, it was a lot of handling pool chemicals, sitting in the scorching heat, applying sunblock, and sweating incessantly beneath my sunglasses. The major downside was having to wear a swimsuit in public, but I was a lifeguard nonetheless, and I was ready to be a hero.

One afternoon, I watched through my generic dark sunglasses as a young family sauntered into the pool area. I was conducting a "lifeguard scan"—the process of systematically scanning the pool with one's eyes. Although some have admitted that they can scan without paying full attention, I caught this new family out of the corner of my eye: two ladies, one older and one younger, and three kids. I can only assume the older one was Grandma. Grandma took the young children into the water while the mom sat with a book in her hand beside the pool.

My eyes scanned to the other part of the pool, and about halfway through the scan on the way back, Grandma's arms began to flail. As the young children looked on, fitted with floaties and enough sunscreen on their noses to cover Ireland, the older woman slipped under the water yet again. The arms never stopped flailing.

This was it. My career as a hero was on the rise. Or so I thought.

I climbed down the lifeguard tower in record time. I am not even sure that my feet hit the pavement before I plunged into the pool. I swam toward the woman who had since come up for air and then fallen back under the water.

When I reached her, I could almost hear the sound of clapping. I saw awards and accolades in my future for saving this woman's life. I am sure there is some kind of Nobel Prize for lifeguards, and I was certain to get one for snatching this woman from the clutches of death.

When I reached her, all but her arms were fully submerged. When I grabbed her, I pushed off the floor of the pool to make sure I had the momentum to get both of us above the water. When I locked eyes with her, I cloaked a smile of smugness. She did not cloak her true feelings, however. Gratitude beyond all measure? Nope. Awe of my strength? Not that either. Awareness of the frailty of life? Negative, Ghostrider.

Disgust? Yep. That's the look I got.

She was trying to make her grandkids giggle and I had ruined her plans. She was not drowning; she was showing off.

When we both caught our breath, she barked at me for being foolish. She chastised me in front of her grandkids for misunderstanding. In indignation, they got out of the pool, packed their things, and marched out of the gates. She left me with the words, "I didn't need your help!"

My wounded pride, soggy bathing suit, and I sat back on the lifeguard chair for the rest of my shift. The words of the woman kept ringing in my chlorinated ears: "I didn't need your help . . ."

In our culture, we commend those who do not need help. Self-sufficiency is of high value, and we often look down at those who are incapable of helping themselves.

Moses and his siblings understood that asking for help, recognizing you cannot do it all on your own, and practicing humility make you strong, not weak.

Moses and Aaron were both humble enough to work in tandem as the leaders of God's people. The two brothers—God's chosen prophet and shepherd, Moses, and God's chosen high priest, Aaron—do not seem to have been threatened by each other's gifts. Moses no doubt was relieved when God called on Aaron to help shoulder the responsibility of speaking on behalf of God.

Throughout their ministries, together and separate, they did not seem to be afraid to let the other shine. During the long journey of the Israelites in the wilderness, Aaron often played a supporting role. An amazing example of this co-leadership was at the battle with the Amalekites.

Read Exodus 17:8-16.

Describe the relationship between Moses and Aaron (and Hur) during this battle.

What might have happened if Aaron and Hur wanted to trade spots with Moses and hold the staff for a while?

What did Moses do after the Israelites defeated the Amalekites? Who got credit for the victory?

I wonder if it was difficult for Moses to be unable to keep his hands raised throughout the battle. To admit that he needed help took great humility and a desire to work in the best interest of God's people. He put others before his own ego and allowed others, including his brother, to help him.

It could not have been easy for Aaron, either. I cannot even lift my arms above my head long enough to French braid my hair, so there is no way I could hold the arms of another for long periods of time, but Aaron and Hur did just that. By the way, Hur was Moses's brother-in-law. I wish everyone's in-laws were so supportive!

My friend Heidi is as close to a superhero as I know. She and her husband are great parents to a small zip code of kids and have a true heart for foster care. They have adopted two kids who came to their home through foster care, and it would not surprise me if God sends them more. She is an amazing resource to other moms when they struggle with foster care, homeschooling, or just keeping their sanity. In one season of their lives, the house they were in was too small to add additional kids to their already busy mix, but she could not shake the responsibility of foster care, so she offered to do laundry for a foster care family instead. She cleaned and folded underwear, bras, and sample-sized clothes in Jesus's name. She is quick to set up Meal Trains for those who are hurting, struggling, or recovering. She has held up the arms for many people, like Aaron did for Moses, when the person was in a battle.

Is it easy or hard for you to ask for help? Explain.

What are the advantages of asking for help?

Are there any drawbacks in asking for help?

When the battle is raging in your life, who are the people you can count on to "raise your hands"? What does that look like in your life?

When have you asked for help recently? Did you receive the help you needed? Explain.

One time, I had to undergo surgery. I did not want anyone to bring my family meals, even though I have taken meals to others a zillion times. It was humbling. I almost found it embarrassing to ask for help. I am comfortable holding up the arms of others, but I am not comfortable asking for help when my arms get tired. That's something God is teaching me.

Read Ecclesiastes 4:9-12 (in the margin).

List the reasons having a friend is better than going it alone.

What is the benefit of having a cord of three strands?

Though it is debated, rabbinic tradition suggests that the author of Ecclesiastes was Solomon, who has been called the wisest man to ever live. In this passage, we certainly see the wisdom in the author's words regarding the value of friendship and of having somebody by your side. Just as this wise person understood the need for others, it's important for you and me to pay attention to his advice.

When we ask for help, work together, and "raise one another's hands," we win the battle. We can help one another up. We can defend one another.

Raise your hands. Ask for help. Be ready to help others, too. We need one another. That's our common ground.

Call to Action

Choose one or more of the following:

- Take action when you can see a need. Walk dogs, clean up yards of elderly neighbors, or help others with their groceries.
- Put a surprise note in someone's lunch box or car.

⁹Two are better than one,
because they have
a good return for
their labor:
¹⁰If either of them falls down,
one can help the
other up.
But pity anyone who falls
and has no one to help
them up.
¹¹Also, if two lie down
together, they will keep
warm.
But how can one keep
warm alone?
¹²Though one may be
overpowered,
two can defend
themselves.
A cord of three strands is not
quickly broken.
(Ecclesiastes 4:9-12)

- Where do you need help? Allow someone to help you.
- Ask God to show you the areas in your life where humility is still an issue.
- Pray for forgiveness and spiritual growth in this area.

Day 5: Teamwork Makes the Dream Work

Scripture Focus

Exodus 18:9-27; Micah 6:4

Today's Key Verses

[17]*Moses' father-in-law replied, "What you are doing is not good.* [18]*You and these people who come to you will only wear yourselves out. The work is too heavy for you; you cannot handle it alone."*

(*Exodus 18:17-18*)

When my parents divorced, my sister and I spent every other weekend with our dad. He always tried to make the time memorable and fun. We spent many an hour at arcades. (Does anyone else remember putting a quarter on the machine to "call" the next game?) We also went to the movies, but our favorite was the go-cart place.

The go-carts were no more than seats strapped to lawn mower motors. Looking back, I am not sure they were safe, but they were *fun*. The perimeter of the track consisted of old car tires, and the course serpentined around the property.

My sister and I spent hours racing against each other. She has always been smaller than I, so she had an advantage, but I was unafraid to keep my foot on the gas pedal without letting up, so that often canceled out her advantage. There was nothing more rewarding than winning. Although younger, my sister beat me in most arenas of competition. She was (and is) a natural athlete. She also was popular. I was neither. On the rare occasion I would win, a smile would decorate my face the rest of the day.

On the track, we were adversaries—unless others joined us.

One day in particular, two brothers entered the track. My sister and I exchanged glances and, without saying a word, we went from adversaries to allies. We were committed to beating those boys. They were our age and undoubtedly sniggered to themselves that two girls were never going to beat them.

But the two girls had every intention of winning.

We knew each other's strengths. The boys had noticed how attractive my sister is, and we knew this could be leveraged.

When the race began, we seemed equally matched. My sister focused in on one of the boys, caught his attention, drew his eyes off the track, and proceeded to run him off the track completely. Then she turned her attention to the other boy while I raced for the finish line. My foot stayed planted on the floor of the cart while my sister's gaze stayed planted on the other brother. When she caught up to him (which she did easily because of her light weight), she drove him off the road, too.

By the time I crossed the finish line, both boys had gotten out of their carts from the sidelines. Both were shaking their heads and, from the looks of it, using language usually reserved for sailors.

We won. But even more, we had worked together to do so. It was the sweetest victory that ever occurred on that track. Teamwork does make the dream work.

Teamwork is a theme in the lives of Moses, Aaron, and Miriam, and it may be the most powerful lesson of all we learn from them.

One of the greatest lessons about teamwork and leadership comes from Moses's father-in-law, Jethro.

Read Exodus 18:9-27. Describe the situation as Jethro saw it.

What did Jethro see as the consequences of this approach of judging?

What was Jethro's solution?

Did Moses take Jethro's advice? Explain.

In what areas of life do you struggle with asking for help?

What has stopped you from asking for help?

Who might you be able to ask for this help?

Although this story does not pertain to the siblings directly, it surely served as a wonderful example for them as they shouldered their separate responsibilities. Finding capable "captains" in your work can be a key to your long-term health and success. Jethro knew that. Moses learned it. You and I need to learn it too.

One famous team in history was called the "Dream Team." In 1992, the US Olympic Men's Basketball Team was truly remarkable: Michael Jordan, Larry Bird, Magic Johnson, Scottie Pippen, Patrick Ewing, Karl Malone, David Robinson, John Stockton, Chris Mullen, Clyde Drexler, Christian Laettner, and Charles Barkley. These men represented some of the greatest players ever. The Dream Team won every game by an average of 43.8 points on their way to the gold medal.[10]

However, the Dream Team was not without its weaknesses. In fact, they lost a scrimmage to a team of college players before they headed into the Olympics.[11] The experience proved humbling and propelled the pros to practice harder and work better together. It is possible that without that battle, the Dream Team may not have lived up to their nickname or won the gold.

What is your favorite sports team?

List some teams you are on right now, such as family, church group, work employees, and volunteer teams. Next to each team, write the names of any of the teammates you feel need help right now, along with ways you can help them. Circle any of the names you have offered to help in the past month.

Teams	Teammates Who Need Help	How I Can Help

Moses, Aaron, and Miriam grew to understand leadership and teamwork. They also recognized they were stronger together. As we've seen, Moses was the shepherd, Aaron was the priest, and Miriam was the prophetess. Moses led the people as God's spokesman, Aaron led them in religious practices, and Miriam led them in worship and knowledge.

Maybe the greatest nod to their teamwork came in the Book of Micah.

Look up Micah 6:4 and write it in the space below:

As we saw on Day 3, Moses, Miriam, and Aaron were not without weaknesses, but their teamwork has earned them a place in our hearts as leaders, pioneers, and examples of those who work hard to find common ground for God's glory. In Micah 6:4, God reminded His people that He brought them out of Egypt and slavery and sent Moses, Aaron, and Miriam to lead them.

Teamwork requires time, a willingness to help others, humility, receptivity to receiving help, practice, and patience. Whether it is on a sports team, around the kitchen table, or in a women's ministry meeting, we are called to live, work, and thrive in community. It takes grit to develop teamwork, but when we work together, God promises His presence and His blessing (Matthew 18:20).

Call to Action

Choose one or more of the following:

- Meditate on verses in God's Word about the importance of working together in unity and harmony. Start with Ecclesiastes 4:9-12; Proverbs 27:17; 1 Corinthians 1:10; Psalm 133:1; and Hebrews 10:24-25.
- Help someone find the positive aspects of her or his current situation.
- Be kind to the people in your everyday "teams"—the people in your family, church groups, and work or volunteer teams. How can you encourage them?
- Learn the names of the other people who contribute in some way to your everyday activities: the security guard in your building, the front desk manager of your office building, the barista at your favorite coffee shop, and so forth. Call them by name. Say hello to strangers and smile as much as possible.
- Pray that God would send you additional "teammates" to help you in your walk with Him.
- Pray that God would reveal places where you have positioned yourself as the judge in the life of another. Pray for forgiveness and healing.

Weekly Wrap-up

As I write this, our country is in a bit of a pickle. Coronavirus, political animosity, racial tension, Facebook brawling, name-calling, rampant "unfriending," arguments about wearing masks, online church, unemployment, murder hornets, wildfires, and weight gain have characterized 2020. Although the weight gain and unemployment affected me most personally, the murder hornets, as they were called, seemed like adding insult to injury after all that has happened.

But some honeybees in Japan figured out how to handle the deadly hornets. A hornet can kill hundreds of bees, but these clever Japanese bees have learned to turn the table on their neighborhood bully. When a hornet enters a hive to attack a bee, it becomes a signal for the rest of the bees to spring (or I guess fly) into action. (They have to do so quickly or the hornet can release pheromones that signal for reinforcements.) A few hundred bees will collect themselves, surround the hornet, and put on their dancing shoes. Well, not really, but they vibrate their wings rapidly (which looks a lot like some moves from Will Smith) and roast the hornet alive with their body heat. The bee collective can generate temperatures of about 115 degrees Fahrenheit for more than thirty minutes. For people in Arizona, that is a brisk summer's day, but for the hornets, it proves deadly.[12]

Honeybees in Japan recognize one of the tenets of common-ground living: We are stronger together. With the help of others, we can do things that no one person can accomplish alone. But honeybees aren't the only ones who have it going on. Our friends Miriam, Aaron, and Moses also show us the importance of working together.

We've seen this week that their skill sets complemented one another, and their commitment to save their people was unwavering. But it was not all happy faces and hand-holding into the sunset.

Moses's humility (Numbers 12:3) gained him favor in the eyes of the Lord, but his insecurity robbed him of the opportunity to be a mouthpiece for his God. Miriam was a prophet (Exodus 15:20) and used her mouth to lead worship, but she used the same mouth to gossip and grumble against her brother (Numbers 12). In that same verse (Exodus 15:20), Miriam is called "Aaron's sister," not Moses's sister—a possible commentary on her occasional undermining of her younger brother. Aaron was a priest and a leader (Exodus 28:1), but he used his leadership to lead people astray to worship a golden calf (Exodus 32:4).

And that wasn't all. Moses was a doubter, Aaron was fickle, and Miriam was a bit power-hungry (not unlike most first borns I know, including myself). Both Moses and Aaron were guilty of unbelief and disobedience at Meribah (Numbers

20:8-11, 13), and both were prohibited from entering Canaan (Numbers 20:12). And let's not forget, our man Moses was a murderer (Exodus 2:11-15).

One of the most encouraging parts of their story is the way they were remembered. Micah chronicled their legacy: "I [God] brought you up out of Egypt / and redeemed you from the land of slavery. / I sent Moses to lead you, / also Aaron and Miriam" (Micah 6:4). In this account, there is no mention of their failings. Not one whiff of bickering, jealousy, unfaithfulness to God, whining, or backbiting. Just the fact that they were sent by God to lead His people. They deserved to keep those bad labels in the annals of history, but God gave them the label of "leaders" instead.

Friend, your mistakes won't be your legacy. Your shortcomings won't be your label. Your past failures don't have to direct your future. You can learn from Moses, Aaron, and Miriam to find common ground with others and embrace humility. You can trust that God has placed you in a position to make a difference. You can remember that none of us is perfect and that we need to appreciate the contributions of others. You can pursue teamwork and celebrate the gifts of others.

Moses, Aaron, and Miriam set the example for us all.

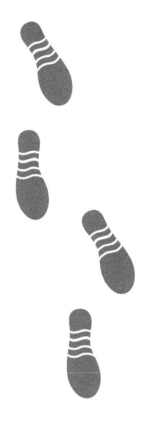

Group Session Guide:
WEEK 2

Moses, Miriam, and Aaron

Working Together Despite Differences

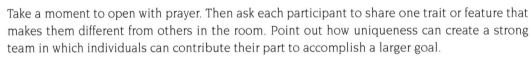

When we find common ground with each other,
we can focus on accomplishing great things for God.

Welcome/Prayer/Icebreaker (5–10 minutes)

Welcome to Session 2 of *Common Ground: Loving Others Despite Our Differences*. This week, we explored the lives of Moses, Miriam, and Aaron and discovered how God used them despite their differences and their faults. Today, we will talk together about changes we can make to become more effective in working with others.

Take a moment to open with prayer. Then ask each participant to share one trait or feature that makes them different from others in the room. Point out how uniqueness can create a strong team in which individuals can contribute their part to accomplish a larger goal.

Video (about 20 minutes)

Play the video segment for Week 2, filling in the blanks as you watch and making notes about anything that resonates with you or that you want to be sure to remember.

Group Session Guide:
WEEK 2

—Video Notes—

Key Scripture: Exodus 14:13-14

_____: "The people"

_____: "Stand firm"

_____: "The Egyptians you see today you will never see again."

_____: "You need only be still."

Other Insights:

Group Discussion (20–25 minutes for a 60-minute session; 30–35 minutes for a 90-minute session)

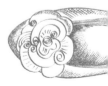

Video Discussion

- Read aloud Exodus 14:13-14. Who is Moses addressing here? How do we see Community, Command, Conquest, and Choice in these verses? (Leader notes: the people, stand firm, God's deliverance and victory over the past, choosing to trust and work together in unity.)

- How does community help us to honor God? Why is working as a team important?
- How would you explain what it means to stand firm? How can we do this in community?
- Why is looking back unhelpful? How can forgiveness help us to move forward?
- What are the things that unite us, and how can we focus on these things together?

Workbook Discussion

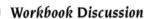

- What are three attributes you possess now that you know come from your background/family of origin? (Day 1, page 48)
- What components of your personality that stem from your upbringing do you wish you could change? Why? (Day 1, page 50)
- What strengths do you have that are direct products of your background? (Day 2, page 55)
- How has God used your weaknesses and flaws?
- To which of the three siblings can you most relate: Moses, with his impatience; Aaron, with his inaction; or Miriam, with her insecurity? Explain. (Day 3, page 63)
- When the battle is raging in your life, who are the people you can count on to "raise your hands"? What does that look like in your life? (Day 4, page 66)
- Who is facing a raging battle in their lives? How can you help them?
- In what areas of life do you struggle with asking for help? What has stopped you from asking for help? (Day 5, page 69)
- How might your asking for help actually benefit the person who is helping you?

Connection Point (10–15 minutes—90-minute session only)

Divide into groups of two to three and discuss the following:

- What cry of your heart is God hearing these days? (Day 2, page 53)
- How might God use friends or family members to answer that cry of your heart?

Closing Prayer (5 minutes)

Close the session by sharing personal prayer requests and praying together. If you like, invite the women to surround those who have shared requests and pray for them aloud. In addition to praying aloud for one another, ask God to help you all learn how to appreciate the different qualities of others and how those traits can be used to build up God's kingdom. Close by thanking God for being a friend who sticks closer than a brother.

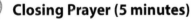

Week 3

Mary, Martha, and Lazarus

Appreciating the Contributions of Others

Memory Verse

*⁴Just as each of us has one body with many members,
and these members do not all have the same function,
⁵so in Christ we, though many, form one body,
and each member belongs to all the others.*
(Romans 12:4-5)

Biblical Background

Jesus had lots of friends, but few outside of the apostles are mentioned as often as Mary, Martha, and Lazarus. All four Gospel writers (Matthew, Mark, Luke, and John) mentioned this sibling trio at least once.

There is no mention of other family members in Mary, Martha, and Lazarus's clan—no parents, spouses, or children are named in any of the accounts. In biblical times, it was unusual for women to remain unmarried. It is possible that the siblings were orphaned and the women had yet to marry. By the way, Jewish women often married at age thirteen or fourteen and men at age eighteen.[1]

I barely had the capacity to get a driver's license at that age, so I cannot imagine getting married and "adulting" at that age! Another possibility is that they were older widows who had not remarried. Or they might have been part of a Jewish sect marked by singleness and celibacy.[2]

Because Martha is often mentioned first among her siblings in the biblical texts, she was probably the oldest. Lazarus is mentioned the least amount, so his more passive role may suggest that he was younger than his sisters.

Some scholars believe the siblings had considerable means since Mary and Martha accommodated Jesus and his disciples on more than one occasion (see Luke 10:38-42 and John 12:2)—a logistic and financial commitment too great for a poor family. In addition, Mary anointed the feet of Jesus with expensive perfume (John 12:1-8), a significant sacrifice that communicated she had the means to do so.

Mary, Martha, and Lazarus lived in Bethany, which interestingly means "House of Poverty" or "House of Affliction" or "House of Dates."[3] Jesus spent much of the last weeks of his life in Bethany. On Palm Sunday, Jesus began his donkey ride into Jerusalem from Bethany (Mark 11:1; Luke 19:29), and He stayed in Bethany the next week (Matthew 21:17; Mark 11:11-12). It is possible that Jesus's last days before His crucifixion were spent in the home of Martha, Mary, and Lazarus. In fact, Jesus ascended into heaven from a place near Bethany (Luke 24:50-51).

In Bible college, I had some wonderful professors who gave great perspective on how best to understand the stories of the Bible. One of them suggested the following when trying to understand a story:

1. Read the whole book in order to get context.
2. Ask, "What did it mean to them?"
3. Ask, "What does it mean to me?"
4. Ask, "What can I glean from this account about the character of God?"

Because the stories of Mary, Martha, and Lazarus are found in all four Gospels, it can be helpful to read all of the accounts in order to better understand the characters and context. As you read, put yourself in each of the accounts. What did the events mean to each of the people in the story? What could the overarching story mean to them? This will give you wonderful insight and a new perspective of these siblings and their interactions with one another and with Jesus. It also will help you glean rich lessons for your own life.

Day 1: Worth Repeating

Today's Key Verses

[41]"Martha, Martha," the Lord answered, "you are worried and upset about many things, [42]but few things are needed—or indeed only one. Mary has chosen what is better, and it will not be taken away from her."

(Luke 10:41-42)

Scripture Focus

Luke 10:38-42

Al Capone and Bugsy Moran. Nikola Tesla and Thomas Edison. Ernest Hemingway and William Faulkner. Michelangelo and Leonardo DaVinci. Do you see a pattern? They are all personal and professional rivals. In every case, their rivalry became famous and, most of the time, fueled them to do greater work. In some cases, however, the rivalry ended badly.

My rival in grade school was Jennifer Roberts. She and I were the tallest girls in our grade. We were both athletes and worked hard in school. We lived in the same neighborhood, came from divorced homes, and wanted to please others. We were both on the pom squad in junior high. We would take turns singing Dolly Parton's part on "Islands in the Stream" (while the other sang Kenny Rogers's part), and we laughed a lot together. She had a cooler name than I did. The name *Jennifer* was so popular in the 1980s—Amberly was not. In my day, the name *Amberly* never graced a mug in a truck stop, while Jennifer could be found on shot glasses, T-shirts, mugs, sunglasses, toiletry items, stickers, and pocket knives in every truck stop in North America. As an adult, I don't care about such things, but back then, this was the litmus test for a great name.

Jennifer and I were friends and spent time together outside of school, but on the softball field, we played on opposite teams—and she was a *slugger*. She could make a softball wish it had never been machine-stitched. Everyone in the league knew how many home runs she hit each week, and my number was always dwarfed by Jennifer's skills with a bat. It was demoralizing.

Some days I prayed she would move away, join the circus, or get injured. I know, the author of a Bible study shouldn't wish harm on another of Jesus's creations, but I wasn't an author then! The truth is, in my young heart of hearts, there were days where what I meant by "get injured" was to be run over by a Mack truck. I did not *really* wish her dead; I just got tired of losing to her—every time.

But my rivalry with Jennifer was also inspiring. Because of her skills, I practiced more and spent more time in the batting cages. She was my rival, but she also stoked the fire in my belly, which made me a better player.

Another famous rivalry in history happened between two sisters. Identical twins Eppie and Pauline were close growing up, but things went sour when they both began work as advice columnists. Eppie gave advice under the pen name "Ann Landers" starting in 1955. Pauline began her career under the moniker of "Dear Abby" in 1956, and tension began to grow.

The rivalry really got ugly when Pauline offered her "Dear Abby" column for less money if the paper would agree to discontinue "Ask Ann" (her sister's column). These two advice columnists were able to give advice regarding interpersonal relationships, but sadly, they were unable to live out the same advice when it came to each other. Their relationship was forever marred after Pauline's offer to the paper. Sources say that even their children are still at odds despite the fact that neither of the twins is still living.[4]

And I thought the Kardashians had some family drama.

I don't think that Mary and Martha were truly *rivals*. I have no reason to doubt that they loved each other and worked together in the home according to the culture of the day,[5] but I imagine that sometimes sparks flew when it came to getting the attention of their friend Jesus.

Read Luke 10:38-42.

Based on what you read, where were each of the women at the time of Jesus's visit?

What was each of the women doing?

What was the tension in the situation, and do you think either sister was "wrong"? Explain.

Can you relate to the tension we find here? I can. Long after Jennifer Roberts and I were rivals, I find myself being jealous of other women in many areas. Mothers who raise kids without raising their voices. Women who can keep a clean house and their sanity concurrently. Wives who seem to successfully balance responsibilities and still prioritize romance (or have the energy for it at the end of the day!). Ladies who can cut out carbs and still be nice to others. Business leaders who lead well and with confidence. Women who can parallel park without a thirty-seven-point turn. Speakers who get the engagements I want. Women who can avoid killing houseplants. Authors who write more books and with a greater degree of success. Women who can wear low-rise jeans. This is a long list, but it is hardly exhaustive.

When it comes down to it, however, I realize that success, fame, peer or professional recognition, and accolades do not fuel my desire for those things. Those things would be great, but when I am truly honest, I become jealous of others because I forget that I already have Jesus's attention. I do not need to succeed in any of those arenas to give God delight. He is not impressed by those things, but I am. I superimpose my false perceptions on Him—largely because of my relationship with my dad. You see, I don't ever think I won the acceptance of my dad. He loved me like crazy, but I never felt like his love was unconditional. So, I spent the rest of his life trying to earn it. And I treat God the same way.

Do you think Martha might have been trying to get Jesus's attention or praise? Explain.

Sometimes, I do things for God to get a gold star on my chart and a holy pat on the back. But that is not how God works. He loves us because we are His. He doesn't love us more when we do good things or love us less when we make bad choices. He just loves us. Completely. Totally. Unconditionally. We cannot earn God's love or attention. We cannot lose it either.

Perhaps the epic battle between these sisters in this scene in Luke 10 would have played out differently if Martha had understood the nature of Jesus's love. My girl Martha was busy with tasks, focused on serving Jesus and the disciples and blessing them with a meal and a place to rest from their travels. She was so confident that she was doing the right thing that she even asked Jesus to recruit her sister to help. And according to cultural tradition, it would not have been customary to ask a guest to settle a family dispute.[6] (Can you imagine a guest doing that at *your* house?) I wonder if, beneath her busy activity, Martha might have wanted attention for her efforts—whether knowingly or unknowingly. Perhaps what she really wanted more than help was a star and a pat on the back from the Son of God.

But He got her attention instead.

Reread Luke 10:40-42.

In what sense did Martha accuse Jesus? (v. 40)

How did Jesus get Martha's attention in verse 41?

Why do you think Jesus said her name twice?

Do you read Jesus's words in verses 41 and 42 as encouragement, instruction, or chastisement? Explain your response.

As a mom, my kids know that if I say their names twice, I am serious. Like DEFCON 1 serious. Like "stop in your tracks and look into my eyeballs" serious. Let's look at some times in the Bible when God or Jesus calls someone by name twice.

Read the following Scriptures. Write down the speaker, the name spoken twice, and the situation in each passage.

Scripture	Speaker	Name Spoken	Situation
Genesis 22:11-13			
Genesis 46:1-4			
Exodus 3:1-10			
1 Samuel 3:1-10			
Luke 22:31-32			
Acts 9:1-6			
Matthew 27:46			

Without exception, these were very important conversations between God and His people. Sometimes, God says our name twice because He needs to get our attention, and what He has to say is important.

I think Jesus said Martha's name twice out of compassion for her. She was cranky and indignant because she was doing the tasks of a woman in her culture, while Mary sat at the feet of Jesus learning, a task usually reserved for men at that time. Jesus wanted her to know He cared, but He had a perspective that she did not. Of course, as the Son of God, He had the luxury of the perspective of heaven. Menial things such as preparing the meal, albeit important, pale in comparison to one growing in the knowledge of God.

Jesus's conversation with Martha was also an important lesson about priorities for *everyone* in the room—Mary, Martha, the disciples, and possibly Lazarus (albeit unmentioned). Even thousands of years later, it is an important lesson for those of us who can relate to Martha at one time or another. We can forget that it is not busyness that makes us accepted. Instead, we need to focus on the One who makes us acceptable to God by His sacrifice.

Do you relate more to Mary or Martha right now? Why?

In what ways are you trying now, or have you tried in the past, to earn the affection and acceptance of God?

How is Jesus trying to get your attention—or how has He gotten your attention in the past?

How would your life be different if you lived each day knowing that you had the acceptance and adoration of Jesus? What would look different than it does now?

If we are going to find common ground with our brothers and sisters in Christ, and find peace within ourselves, we must put aside our judgment of others' relationship with Jesus, keep our focus on Him, and remember that we don't have to earn His attention and affection. Not ever! We are completely loved just as we are—without striving, accomplishing, performing, or achieving. *You* are completely and unconditionally loved simply because you're His.

Call to Action

Choose one or more of the following:

- Rest from busyness by taking a walk and looking for God's handiwork in nature.
- Find a way to bless someone else by something you are able to do as part of your ordinary routine, such as paying for someone's dinner check or cooking an extra portion of dinner or dessert for someone who needs it.
- Look for a humble and simple way to serve. Contact your church and find out if there is a veteran or an elderly member who needs a ride for his or her medical appointments or trips to the grocery store.
- Pray for God to show you how He sees you. Ask that His great love for you would allow you to see others through His eyes.

Day 2: Keeping Jesus in Our Sights

Scripture Focus

John 12:1-11

Today's Key Verses

⁷"Leave her alone," Jesus replied. "It was intended that she should save this perfume for the day of my burial. ⁸You will always have the poor among you, but you will not always have me."

(John 12:7-8)

As my fortieth birthday approached, my husband, Scott, and I were going through some stuff. As if turning forty was not already heavy on my mind (and the wrinkles growing heavy in the corners of my eyes), ministry was especially difficult. There were some leadership issues at the church where Scott was on staff, and it was breaking his heart and spirit. Scott loved the people so much, but the tumult in the office was palpable, and the stress of work was affecting our marriage and our friendships.

You can imagine my delight when some friends invited us over for dinner. As usual, it had taken some strategic planning to coordinate a day that would work for four busy adults. But on the very day of the dinner, Scott and I had made the tearful, difficult decision to leave the church, and we wanted to tell these close friends first. The news we would be bringing to these beloved friends was so heavy on my heart that I hardly got ready. I threw on some sweatpants and a sweatshirt, wrestled my curly hair into a messy bun, and removed the tear streaks from my face. I decided not to add any makeup or even wash my face. I looked like I needed roadside assistance.

What I did not know, however, was that almost one hundred people were waiting at the house of our friends to celebrate my fortieth birthday (three weeks early). They all looked fantastic—donned in party wear and smiles—while I looked like a garage sale. The whole garage.

When they shouted "Surprise!" I nearly threw up. My mom was from the South, and she taught me that a lack of graciousness was not an option; so I put on the bravest face in the history of parties. I smiled so hard my cheeks hurt, but it was my heart that was really hurting. The party was thrown in my honor by loving friends, but I had much more on my mind than cake and ice cream (although as I recall, those were pretty delicious that night).

When was the last time you were really surprised?

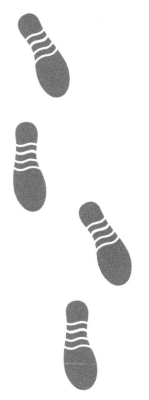

In one of the most critical weeks of His life, Jesus returned to Bethany and spent the evening with friends. They, too, were honoring a friend with a dinner, but the gravity of what would happen in the days and hours to come was no surprise to Jesus.

Have you ever played hide-and-seek? Although God is not trying to hide anything, I always find new things when I do a little "digging" into a passage.

Read John 12:1-11 (on page 86) and do the following:

Circle WHEN this event occurred.

Underline WHERE it occurred.

Place a small star near WHO was there (all of the people).

Highlight or draw a box around the WORDS of Jesus.

What attributes of God/Jesus are displayed in this passage?

Did you notice anything new while studying this account?

¹Six days before the Passover, Jesus came to Bethany, where Lazarus lived, whom Jesus had raised from the dead. ²Here a dinner was given in Jesus' honor. Martha served, while Lazarus was among those reclining at the table with him. ³Then Mary took about a pint of pure nard, an expensive perfume; she poured it on Jesus' feet and wiped his feet with her hair. And the house was filled with the fragrance of the perfume.

⁴But one of his disciples, Judas Iscariot, who was later to betray him, objected, ⁵"Why wasn't this perfume sold and the money given to the poor? It was worth a year's wages." ⁶He did not say this because he cared about the poor but because he was a thief; as keeper of the money bag, he used to help himself to what was put into it.

⁷"Leave her alone," Jesus replied. "It was intended that she should save this perfume for the day of my burial. ⁸You will always have the poor among you, but you will not always have me."

⁹Meanwhile a large crowd of Jews found out that Jesus was there and came, not only because of him but also to see Lazarus, whom he had raised from the dead. ¹⁰So the chief priests made plans to kill Lazarus as well, ¹¹for on account of him many of the Jews were going over to Jesus and believing in him.

(John 12:1-11)

Martha served the meal again (big surprise). Again, Mary did not help her, but it seems Martha had grown in understanding since the last dinner with Jesus. There is no account of Martha's frustration with her sister this time. What a wonderful encouragement that we actually see a clue of the likely growth in Martha's life. Although her body was performing the same tasks, her heart had apparently changed. Both women were doing their best to honor Jesus.

Lazarus was reclining at the table with Jesus. I have always wondered what that looked like. I take food so seriously, I cannot imagine reclining while eating—I would spill half of the meal down my shirt! I am usually so excited about dinner that I would stand and dance if I could. In the Old Testament, a leather mat placed on the floor often served as a table.[7] Meals in the New Testament were a little different. Men would lie on a *triclinium*, which was a U-shaped couch that sat low to the ground. They would lean toward the center where a table of food was placed. Guests would prop on one arm and eat with the other, their legs stretched out behind them.[8] Lazarus got to hang out with the Son of the Living God. He was doing his best to listen to Jesus.

Then Mary did something extraordinary. She took a container of pure nard (or spikenard) and anointed Jesus's feet. In ancient times, nard was an ointment used as a perfume of great value.[9] Some scholars think it was Mary's dowry or her inheritance.[10] It was worth a year's wages, which is especially important to remember since women did not often work outside of the home in those days.[11]

I cannot imagine. I do not use perfume that often. When I do, it is cheap— usually a gift from my daughter or a freebie that comes with a purchase of something else. What Mary did was more than offer Jesus the opportunity to smell good. She honored him. She sacrificed what could have been her dowry for the worship of Jesus and wiped his feet with her hair. In biblical times, no honorable woman would ever be seen in public with her hair down, but this custom was unimportant to her because she was so focused on Jesus.[12] She was doing her best to worship Him.

What is your favorite perfume? Why?

Read 2 Corinthians 2:14 and paraphrase it below.

According to this verse, what are we used by God to do?

This meal provided the backdrop for the rest of the week. This dinner honored Jesus while the religious leaders of the day were scheming to dishonor Him (John 12:10-11). The food that Martha served Jesus that night sustained Him while He was entering the city for Passover and palm branches were lifted to

Him (John 12:12-19). The conversation with Lazarus and the disciples at the table was probably fresh on the mind of Jesus as Judas betrayed Him (John 18:1-5). The nard with which Mary anointed Jesus's feet with was still in his pores as He was led to Golgotha to be crucified (John 19:4-22).

In John 12, these siblings focused on Jesus. Not the service of Martha. Not the security of Lazarus. Not the sacrifice of Mary. They had watched as Jesus conquered death and raised Lazarus from the dead—they knew He deserved their full attention.

If we want to find common ground with one another, we must regularly and humbly remember that we are placed on the earth to bring glory to Jesus. All of our tasks, talents, and treasures are about Him. We can serve alongside one another, adding our own contributions, while ultimately pointing to the One who deserves all the credit.

I attended a wedding where the bride and groom, two genetically perfect people, threw a near-perfect event. It was a wedding worthy of Pinterest posts. Even the food was perfect. The caterer was someone who knew the family and had a gift for all things culinary, and the food did not disappoint.

That being said, the reason I wrote "near-perfect event" was because of that caterer. After the fathers of both the bride and groom gave articulate, heartfelt speeches that left the audience delighted and a little weepy (like a well-written television drama), something weird happened.

The caterer insisted on giving a speech. The caterer. He grabbed the mic and proceeded to go on and on (and on . . .) about the food and his relationship to the bride and groom.

He successfully stopped the wedding festivities in their tracks.

He chose to make the event about him. His contribution. His relationships. His food. He missed the point completely. He took the focus off of the bride and groom (and their love) and made it about himself.

Who in your life keeps Jesus as the center of attention, from your vantage point?

When you were a kid, what brought you the most amount of attention?

Where do you find yourself "grabbing the mic" of attention?

What are some ways that you give Jesus attention on a daily basis?

At this meal, Martha served without bringing attention to her hard work. Lazarus spent time with Jesus but did not bring attention to how close he was to Jesus or how carefully He listened. Mary washed Jesus's feet with her hair, using her greatest material possession, but she did not bring attention to her contribution. They all gave credit where it was due. They all brought attention to Jesus.

If we want to find common ground with one another, we must resist the temptation to grab the mic of attention. When we focus on giving Jesus our attention, our admiration, and our accolades, unity is downright attainable—even if we don't agree on much else!

Call to Action

Choose one or more of the following:

- Keep your focus on Jesus by volunteering at your church or other faith-based nonprofit.
- If you attend a party decorated with flowers, offer to take the flowers to a nursing home and deliver them to the residents or nurses there.
- In the next week, commit to spending an extra ten minutes each day just resting and listening in God's presence.
- Pray for God to show you places where you "take the mic" and the attention off Jesus. Ask God to help you shift your focus to Jesus.

Day 3: I Am Happy for You

Today's Key Verses

[25]Jesus said to her, "I am the resurrection and the life. Whoever believes in me will live, even though they die. [26]Everyone who lives and believes in me will never die. Do you believe this?"

(John 11:25-26 CEB)

Scripture Focus

John 11:1-44

My sister, Allyson, has an impeccable sense of fashion, design, and taste. She always smells good too. Yep. Even when money was tight as a teenager, she would spend her hard-earned shekels on perfume. One of my favorites was a cologne for women called "Paloma Picasso"; it smelled like a million dollars in unmarked bills on my sister. When she would wear that perfume and walk through a room, I swear I could hear olfactory angels singing. She smelled *a-maz-ing*.

One evening, I was getting ready for a date, feeling a little less than beautiful. I thought some of her perfume would be the magic elixir to blind my date from seeing the acne that had cropped up that afternoon. My sister was not home to ask permission, and frankly, she had borrowed my clothes a hundred billion times without asking, so I felt justified in stealing a few drops.

Those who use expensive perfume know that quality perfume mixes with the body's pheromones to create a unique scent for the wearer. Those of us who think five dollars is a lot to spend on perfume do not know this secret, so I had no idea that this perfume would smell differently on me than it did on my sister. As my date rang the doorbell, I hurriedly applied the *eau de toilette* behind each ear and on each wrist and headed out the door.

Being a gentleman, my date opened the car door for me. When I got in the small, enclosed space, I thought something had died therein. It smelled like a mixture of old cheese and gym socks. And I do not mean *clean* gym socks.

I thought to myself, "Wow, poor guy. I had heard that teenage boys can be clueless, but does he not know that his car smells like poor choices and mold?"

And then it hit me. It was not his car that reeked. It was *me*.

My *eau de toilette* had turned into just *toilette* in minutes.

Before he made his way around the car and got in, I quickly did a test sniff on my wrists. Yep. It was me. The perfume had mixed with my body chemistry and created a new scent altogether—*eau de rancid*.

The date did not last long, and I never borrowed my sister's perfume again. Lesson learned.

In today's Scripture, smell is a minor character in the story.

Read John 11:1-7.

What news did Jesus hear?

What can we deduce about Jesus's relationship with these siblings from these verses?

The first few verses give us a glimpse into the relationship Jesus shared with Mary, Martha, and Lazarus. The women sent a message telling Jesus that "the one you love is sick" (v. 3). By the way, to be known as the one loved by Jesus is pretty fantastic. And the good news is, we can all say that about ourselves. You will never meet a person Jesus does not love.

Even though Jesus clearly loved Lazarus, He did go not to Bethany immediately so He could heal His friend. He stayed where He was for two more days. I imagine how confused the disciples must have been. I've been in their shoes—and so have you. Even though Jesus loves us deeply and fiercely, He does not always respond to our problems as quickly as we want Him to. He doesn't always heal immediately. He does not always alleviate our pain. But as we will discover in this story, God's purposes and plans are always bigger than we could ever understand.

Read John 11:11-15.

What did Jesus call "death" in verse 11?

What communication gap do you see in verses 11-13?

According to verse 14, why was Jesus glad he was not in Bethany at the time of Lazarus's death?

I love the disciples because I am so much like them. Jesus spoke truth to them, but they didn't understand. They were thinking, "Take two aspirin and eat some chicken noodle soup," while Jesus knew that no amount of soup would help Lazarus get better. At least Jesus gave them hints that something big was just around the corner.

Read John 11:17-37.

Put yourself in this story as a bystander. What do you see? hear? feel? taste? touch? How are you moved by the actions of the people you are watching?

Lazarus had been in the tomb for four days, undeniably deceased according to Jewish custom and common sense. Mary and Martha, clearly loved by the people who came to comfort them, mourned in their own unique ways. Mary chose to stay at home. Martha, on the other hand, went out to meet Jesus and, in the process, made some staggering claims about Him.

Look again at John 11:21-27. What claims did Martha make? How was her faith in Jesus different from her sister's?

The actions of the women seem like a juxtaposition from earlier interactions with Jesus. Mary had worshipped and Martha had followed customs. In John 11, Martha's faith took center stage. She declared Jesus as "the Messiah, the Son of God, who is to come into the world" (v. 27). Her bold statement mirrors Peter's declaration in Matthew 16:16: "You are the Messiah, the Son of the living God." Not bad company to be in!

After Martha spoke to Jesus, she "called her sister Mary aside" (v. 28) and told her Jesus was looking for her. What a tender Savior, close to the brokenhearted (Psalm 34:18). And Mary came running out to meet Him.

Reread John 11:28-32.

What did Mary declare to Jesus? Where have you heard this statement before?

What tone do you hear in her words? (There's no right or wrong answer.)

What did Mary's statement reveal about her relationship with Jesus?

The interaction of the women with Jesus sparked a conversation between some of the Jews who were there. I love being an armchair quarterback when I watch my favorite team, but I cannot imagine making my comments if the coach was sitting in the next room. Yet, the Jews who were there questioned why Jesus didn't intervene (v. 37). They questioned the Savior of the world. Yikes!

John 11:35 is the shortest verse in the Bible, but do not skim past these two important words: "Jesus wept." In the verses that follow, we see that Jesus expressed deep emotion at least one more time (v. 38). This verse is followed by one of the more comical ones. Jesus commanded that the stone be rolled away from Lazarus's grave. The ever-practical Martha responded, "But Lord…by this time there is a bad odor, for he has been there four days" (v. 39).

Translation: "I don't think you want to do that because the grave reeks!"

Undeterred, Jesus's compassion and care for His people moved Him to action. He raised Lazarus from the dead with a loud voice (v. 43). I do most things with a loud voice, so I totally love that description; but even with my volume, I cannot always get my kids to come out of their rooms for dinner; Jesus made Lazarus come out of the grave! *Wow.*

Many came to faith in Jesus because of this incident (v. 45). And the miracle of this resurrection reverberated through the town and throughout history.

Each of the three siblings played a part in the story that God unfolded in John 11. Martha gained insight on the identity of Jesus, Mary got encouragement, and Lazarus got to breathe again. Each played a vital role and allowed the other two the space to grow without getting in the way.

I still love my sister's scent when we see each other. Although she does not wear the same perfume anymore, I still celebrate her. No envy, not a desire to become her, just a celebration of who she is.

As we read earlier in the week, we spread the fragrance of the knowledge of Christ (2 Corinthians 2:14). Martha shared the scent of Christ when she verbalized a claim about who He is. Mary shared the scent of Christ by displaying what a heart bowed in worship looks like. Lazarus shared the scent of Christ when he listened to and obeyed the voice of Jesus, coming out of the tomb.

How are *you* sharing the scent of the knowledge of Christ?

Call to Action

Choose one or more of the following:

- How can you share the fragrance of Christ by getting involved—or more involved—in the church? Serve alongside fellow believers and celebrate the sweet-smelling contributions of others.
- Thank your pastors for the ways they spread the fragrance of Christ.
- Share a book about Jesus with someone who might appreciate the "aroma" of its message and be drawn closer to Christ.
- Pray for God to place people in your path with whom you can share the joy of a life lived for Christ. Pray for boldness to do so.

Day 4: Has Anyone Got Change?

Today's Key Verses

[16]*From now on we regard no one from a worldly point of view. Though we once regarded Christ in this way, we do so no longer.* [17]*Therefore, if anyone is in Christ, the new creation has come: The old has gone, the new is here!*

(2 Corinthians 5:16-17)

I wore tight, pink leopard pants. I listened to really loud, guitar-heavy music. My hair contained enough hairspray to be registered as a lethal weapon. I dated concert photographers, wore heavy metal T-shirts, went to rock concerts, hung out with the "stoners" (although drugs were not my thing), used profanity like it was a class in school, and wore enough eyeliner to supply any small country. My circle of friends made fun of the "popular kids," but we were all jealous of them.

I always got along with all types of folks. I was an athlete, so I could hang out with my teammates. I was a good student, so I could always fit in at a study session. I have always been loud, so I got along swimmingly with those in the drama department.

But I was never in the popular group. They all had nice cars, while we called my Toyota a POJ2000. The POJ stood for "piece of junk." (In all honesty, that is not *exactly* the terminology I used.) The popular kids all dressed well. I was too interested in comfort to maintain that for any length of time. Plus, I did not have that kind of money.

I did observe one thing about how to get in with the popular kids: they drank beer on the weekends. This is a royal overexaggeration, but at the time, I was confident in my assessment. So, at the end of my sophomore year, I threw a keg party at my apartment. My dad was staying with his girlfriend for the weekend and left me alone in the two-bedroom abode. I made flyers, invited every popular kid I knew, and bought all the alcohol I could get my hands on. I have never looked my age, which was wonderful when I was sixteen and everyone would guess I was twenty-five. Now at age fifty, I no longer consider it an advantage.

I just knew this party would make me friends.

As people arrived, I reminded them of the party rule: "If you drink, you stay." I did not want anyone driving intoxicated, so I planned to have everyone crash at my apartment that evening. Over one hundred teens showed up, filling every corner, nook, and cranny of the apartment in no time.

After much consumption, laughter, and frivolity, things began to calm down around 2:00 a.m. The inebriated bodies of students were strewn all over the place. But so were red cups. They occupied every inch of floor space not covered by students.

I started to pick up those cups to throw them away. As I did, I lamented that even though the party brought a lot of the most popular kids to my house, no one asked about me or engaged me in conversation. No one asked if they could help clean up. I was no closer to popularity than before and I certainly had not gained even one friend. I began to cry. It was a soft cry at first, but then it grew into a deeper, more guttural cry quickly. I was lonely and disappointed. My plan had failed miserably, and all I gained was the cost of having the carpets cleaned. Cup after cup served as a reminder of my loneliness and failure.

That night took me back to a time many years before when I had responded to a sermon about Jesus coming to earth so that we could be friends with God. I had not understood it all at the time, but I had responded to that altar call because I wanted a friendship with God. A nice man had prayed with me about becoming a follower of Jesus, and I had been baptized a few weeks later. But without training or follow-up, I quickly had forgotten about Jesus.

As I cleaned up the apartment, I remembered that decision I'd made. My desire to be friends with God was rekindled once again. I did not know any fancy words or prayer, but in the middle of my living room, surrounded by drunk teens and party debris, and with red Solo cups in my hand, I cried out to Jesus. I surrendered my life fully to Him.

Things did change after that. I moved back in with my mom, transferred to a different high school, dressed differently, and started attending church regularly. My transformation was so radical that when students from my old high school came in contact with me, they did not recognize me even if I called them by name. I heard of at least one interaction where someone from my old school described me, and someone from my new school said, "Must be a different Amberly. Your description sounds nothing like her."

Sometimes, we label people and then refuse to see any change in them. Or we feel limited by our own past choices and other people's perceptions of us because of those choices.

If we want to find common ground on the battleground of disagreement, we must refrain from putting labels on others and thus disregard the work God is doing in their lives. Instead, we need to affirm how God sees people.

Read the following verses, and next to each verse, write the "label" believers are given.

Ephesians 2:10

1 Peter 2:9

John 1:12

John 15:5

John 15:15

1 Corinthians 6:19

1 Corinthians 12:27

2 Corinthians 5:17

Which one of them is your favorite? Why?

From what you know of God's Word, are there additional labels believers are called? List below any that come to mind:

If we were to label Mary, Martha, and Lazarus, Mary might be labeled "the worshipper." She sacrificed her perfume and washed the feet of Jesus. She ignored the social norms of domestic responsibilities when given the opportunity to glean from the Master. She learned at Jesus's feet, a place usually reserved for men.

Martha could have been considered "the dutiful servant." She opened her home to Jesus and some of His followers (and possibly some of their friends) and served them well. Her actions were not bad, but early on, her attitude was flawed. She is best known for her acts of service, not an attitude of submission.

Lazarus no doubt became known as "the guy Jesus raised from the dead." His name is not mentioned nearly as much as his sisters', but the account of his resurrection is probably the thing for which Lazarus is most known. (It's kind of unforgettable!)

What do you think you are most known for? (Good cook, loud laugh, artist, other)

Do you think that label is accurate? Explain.

Jesus saw more in Mary, Martha, and Lazarus than a label or behavior.

He saw Mary as more than a ministry partner or servant. Being hospitable was the duty of a woman in the culture at that time, but Jesus saw her as a valued follower. He broke through the rules placed on her by society and culture and allowed her to take the posture of a disciple. He defended her when Judas questioned her choice of pouring out nard and affirmed that her actions would be remembered wherever the gospel is preached (Matthew 26:13; Mark 14:9).

Jesus saw Martha as more than a hostess. He saw her as a proclaimer of truth. She made some of the most profound statements concerning the identity of Jesus, even before the disciples did. She rightfully called Him the "Messiah, the Son of God, who is to come into the world" (John 11:27) at a time in history when the word of a woman would not stand up in court.

Jesus saw Lazarus as more than a dinner guest at the home of his sisters. He saw Lazarus as a friend and disciple and a person through whom He could display the resurrection power of God. Although Lazarus became the target of the plot of the chief priests after Jesus raised him from the dead (John 12:10-11), God protected him from harm.

Due to COVID-19, I lost a job I adored. I loved the people alongside whom I served. I was passionate about the mission and purpose of the organization. I loved the things I was learning. The loss was devastating. Although I knew that the organization could not handle the crushing financial blow COVID dished out without making hard decisions, I did not expect to be one of those hard decisions. Many people lost their jobs that day, but I still felt so isolated and dejected. Although I know in my head that I was not let go because of poor work performance on my part, my heart has yet to get that memo.

I had never lost a job before. I did not know how to respond. Most of my coworkers who remained did not know how to respond either. It was an awkward "dance" when I saw one of them in the local grocery store. Mostly, I just felt defeated. I felt like *everyone* I came in contact with somehow magically *knew* that I was a loser because I had lost my job. I labeled myself a loser. A failure. A disappointment. Inadequate. I put those labels on myself.

I still struggle not to label myself every day, if not with the labels I mentioned, then with labels such as the "not enoughs"—not smart enough, not capable enough, not educated enough, not doing enough, and so forth. Although I am now doing really meaningful work I enjoy, I still feel labeled by that one loss.

Have you ever been given a negative label by others—or yourself? Loser? Disappointment? Not good enough? Irrelevant? How did you feel when receiving that label?

[13]You also were included in Christ when you heard the message of truth, the gospel of your salvation. When you believed, you were marked in him with a seal, the promised Holy Spirit, [14]who is a deposit guaranteeing our inheritance until the redemption of those who are God's possession—to the praise of his glory.
(Ephesians 1:13-14)

Have you ever labeled others because of their flaws and then "trapped" them there without giving them space to grow? Explain.

Before I was even born, Jesus saw me. He saw past the big hair and leopard pants and saw who I really am: His redeemed child. He does not put negative labels on me. He does not see me as a loser. He does not remind me of all the poor choices and past mistakes I have made over the past fifty years. I do enough of that to myself. Instead, He loves me so much that He continues to grow me into more of His likeness each day (which, by the way, takes a lot of patience on His part).

Although we looked at some images that could be considered "labels" for those of us who follow Christ, there's really only one label or "mark" Jesus sees on each of us.

Read Ephesians 1:13-14 in the margin.

According to these verses, what kind of mark does God place on you when you become a believer? (v. 13)

Based on these verses, what other mark or label would describe you? (v. 14)

Since I was a child, I have been told that my optimistic outlook is "seeing the world through rose-colored glasses." Perhaps you've heard that phrase. It may be true about how we sometimes see things and people, but God does not see us through "rose-colored glasses." Instead, He sees us through "scarlet-colored glasses." He sees us through the blood of His Son. He sees us through the lens of His love, redemption, and grace. When we follow God, He marks us with a seal—the Holy Spirit. In New Testament times, a seal wasn't just a sticker on the back of an envelope. It gave value to something. It was a token of ownership. It also signified authenticity and validity to a document.[13]

Do you see the significance for you and me? The only label that matters, the only label that ultimately defines us, is the label "God's beloved." He has stamped us as His possession. *You are His.* And nothing will ever change that, not even your worst day on this planet.

I wish you and I could see ourselves and others through scarlet-colored glasses long enough for those labels to lose their stickiness and fall away. I want to be able to see others as God does. If we want to find common ground with other believers, we need to shed the outdated labels others have given us and let go of the labels we have given to others.

Take a page from the playbook of Jesus. Remember that you grow and change. And so do others.

Call to Action

Choose one or more of the following:

- One way to drop labels we give others is to serve others. Volunteer at a homeless shelter.
- Tell someone the truth about the labels you have wrongly placed on him or her. Ask for his or her forgiveness.
- Invite someone to dinner, especially during the holidays when people can feel especially alone—and perhaps "labeled."
- Pray that God would help you hold captive negative thoughts. Pray that He would give you the courage and strength to drop labels others have thrust upon you.

Day 5: Attitude Adjustments

Today's Key Verses

⁶Do not be anxious about anything, but in every situation, by prayer and petition, with thanksgiving, present your requests to God. ⁷And the peace of God, which transcends all understanding, will guard your hearts and your minds in Christ Jesus.

(Philippians 4:6-7)

Scripture Focus

Luke 10:38-42

At Disneyland, one of my favorite rides is Big Thunder Mountain. It is a family-friendly roller coaster that first opened back in 1979. It has been around forever. We often break the rules and ride the train sideways. We face the other person in the car (it is so fun!), giggle like schoolgirls at a BTS or Jonas Brothers concert, and point out with fondness all the cheesy, frontier-themed elements on the ride.

My favorite part of the experience is the announcement that precedes the adventure. A pleasant voice with a country twang pronounces a zillion rules (probably because of rabble-rousers who ride the train sideways) and then says the following: "This here's the wildest ride in the wilderness."

In my experience, that is just not true. Ministry is the wildest ride in the wilderness.

Yes, ministry. I love Jesus, but full-time ministry is not an amusement park ride. Scott and I have had the privilege of being part of some of the most dynamic, transformative church and parachurch organizations on the planet. We have seen God do some incredible work in us, through us, around us, and despite us over the years. We have served alongside some amazing men and women of God who love Him and love others so well.

But like all humans who work with other humans, we also have served alongside some less than stellar characters. And we have made mistakes along the way. We have our own issues to our tissues and bring those into the ministries of which we have been a part.

Ministry can be downright *hard*. It does not require the mental rigors of rocket science, but it takes people science. Not the manual rigors of construction, but the construction of communities. Not the emotional rigors of a crisis therapist, but it sure can feel like it. I am not alone in my feelings on the subject. According to some recent polls by full-time ministry leaders, "90 percent of pastors report the ministry was completely different than what they thought it would be like," and "35 percent of pastors battle depression or fear of inadequacy."[14]

These statistics are heartbreaking to me, mostly because ministers say they are discouraged, dissatisfied, disconnected, and disengaged. These are not adjectives that should be used to describe the profession that introduces Jesus to a hurting world.

But those in full-time ministry are not alone. People in healing and helping professions also struggle with difficulties. For instance, 92 percent of nurses report moderate to very high levels of work-related stress.[15] Trash collectors have a higher mortality rate than police officers, construction workers, and miners.[16] Up to 37 percent of firefighters meet the criteria for PTSD.[17] More than 40 percent of teachers leave their profession within the first five years of their careers.[18] According to a Gallup poll, stay-at-home moms experience more sadness, anger, worry, depression, and less happiness than their employed peers.[19] And the list goes on.

No matter the career path, *all* of us will face hardships, struggles, discord, interpersonal strife, and stress.

On this last day of our study of Mary, Martha, and Lazarus, I want to unpack some of the pitfalls one of these three faced so that we can avoid falling into the same pits ourselves. I would like to focus on Martha. She is the eldest, the boldest, and the bossiest. She is, well, me. Don't judge. I am guessing you can be a Martha sometimes, too.

Let's look again at the story in Luke 10:38-42. Read it below.

³⁸*While they were traveling, [Jesus] entered a village, and a woman named Martha welcomed him into her home.* ³⁹*She had a sister named Mary, who also sat at the Lord's feet and*

was listening to what he said. ⁴⁰*But Martha was distracted by her many tasks, and she came up and asked, "Lord, don't you care that my sister has left me to serve alone? So tell her to give me a hand."*

⁴¹*The Lord answered her, "Martha, Martha, you are worried and upset about many things,* ⁴²*but one thing is necessary. Mary has made the right choice, and it will not be taken away from her."* **(CSB)**

How would you describe Martha's emotional state, and why?

How would you describe her state of mind, and why?

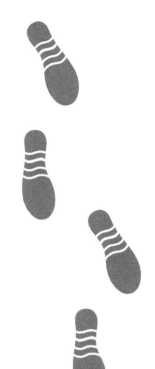

I see at least three adjectives that describe Martha in Luke 10:38-42. These often reflect how many who serve the Lord feel in their work.

1. Martha was distracted.

I once heard a story about the building of the Taj Mahal, and although I have been unable to verify the historical accuracy of the story, I'd like to share it here as a poignant fable. The story goes that the grand structure was a monument built by the Mughal emperor Shah Jahan for the remains of his favorite wife, Mumtaz Mahal. During the construction of the opulent and costly structure, Shah Jahan was overseeing the construction of the memorial when he came across an old box of construction materials, and he asked for all of it to be disposed of so as not to dishonor his wife with debris and disorder. It is said that his beloved wife's remains, for whom he was constructing the Taj Mahal, were contained inside the box and were discarded as per Shah Jahan's orders. He had become so obsessed with the building itself that he had lost sight of the reason he was building it.

While the story is probably untrue, it still knocks my teeth out.

We have all been involved in a project, plan, cause, committee, or group that lost sight of its original vision or mission. We have all become tired, distracted, frustrated, discouraged, and "hangry" (or is it just me?), causing us to lose sight of why we were doing a project in the first place.

I have reached the stage in my life in which I forget why I went into a room. I know I had a reason to go to that room. I get to said room and then just scan the room for a reason I was headed there. I even talk aloud, "I am here for something and I know that eventually, I will remember why." It is maddening. Sometimes I remember and sometimes I do not.

I had a coworker whose job description included answering the phones. Although she had other duties, the main one was to treat people kindly on the phone and answer any questions they might have. One day, I asked her how her day was going. She said, "Okay, but I would get a lot more done if people would just stop calling." She got busy with side jobs and forgot the very reason she was there.

In the story in Luke 10:38-42, we see that Martha forgot why she was preparing food. She remembered that there were lots of hungry people. She remembered her cultural duty to entertain. She remembered that an important guest was in her house, but she forgot to stop and truly focus on Him. She got distracted.

"But Martha was distracted by all the preparations that had to be made" (Luke 10:40a). In the Greek, the word *distracted* is *periespao*, which can be translated "being dragged in different directions."[20]

Given the statistics about civil servants, ministry leaders, and stay-at-home moms, I am guessing that many of them have gotten distracted, too. They have been dragged in different directions and have felt the strain of it—as no doubt their families have too.

The 21st Century King James Version (KJ21) reads, "But Martha was *encumbered with much serving*" (v. 40, emphasis added). If we do not keep our eyes on Jesus, it is easy to become distracted, weighed down, and overcome by the tasks at hand. It happened to Martha. It has happened to me. Perhaps it has happened to you, too.

What is dragging your attention in different directions right now?

What in your life is taking your eyes off the most important priorities?

Read 1 Corinthians 9:24-25. How would you describe what it means to "run in such a way as to get the prize"?

2. Martha was isolated.

In verse 40, Martha said, ""Lord, do you not care that my sister has left me to serve alone? Tell her then to help me" (ESV). In the Interlinear Bible (a version that shows side by side the Greek or Hebrew words used for the English translation), the two words on either side of *alone* are the same: *me*. It literally reads "me alone me."[21] Martha felt left out and left alone, even though her house was full of people. And she was not having it. I suspect that she and Mary had become accustomed to working in tandem. But on this occasion, with Mary at the feet of Jesus, getting a chance to listen to the Master, Martha was left to figure things out herself. Or so she thought.

I do not like to be alone. When I am traveling, I often turn on the television where I am staying, so I can drown out the feeling of being by myself. For some, lots of solitude helps them recharge and reboot. For me, alone time is like water torture. I would rather try on bathing suits than to be left alone for a whole day!

One of the most dangerous feelings is that of being *truly* alone and isolated, especially in times of pain. "No one understands me." "No one even cares." "No one will miss me if I am gone." "No one has gone through this." These are common cries of hurting people. Isolation in the midst of pain adds insult to injury. It is like an accelerant to the hurt.

Read Psalm 34:17-20. What do these verses promise about God?

Now read Joshua 1:9, and write it in your own words below:

What do these two passages say about God? About you?

Have you ever felt isolated or alone? What was that like?

Martha seems to have felt distant from her guests and from her sister and even from Jesus. And I think her emotions propelled her to get indignant with the Savior of the world: "Lord, don't you care . . ." (v. 40). I feel like the angels in the heavenly realms all gasped when she said that. It was reality TV before the television was invented. Her statement was real and raw. (But Jesus could handle it!)

Maybe that is why Jesus said her name twice—to remind her of who she was and to communicate value to her. To remind her that she was not alone or forgotten. And neither are you.

3. Martha was anxious.

In Luke 10:41, Jesus calls our girl on the carpet with grace and tenderness, but with truth nonetheless:

> "Martha, Martha," the Lord answered, "you are worried and upset about many things." (NIV)

> Jesus answered and said to her, "Martha, Martha, you are worried and troubled about many things." (NKJV)

> The Lord answered her, "Martha, Martha, you are anxious and troubled about many things." (ESV)

> The Master said, "Martha, dear Martha, you're fussing far too much and getting yourself worked up over nothing." (MSG)

I will admit that when entertaining at our house, I stress out about every detail. I want everything to be fantastic for the guests, but sometimes in my preparation for their arrival, I get downright aggravated. My family clearly does not move (or clean or cook or breathe) at the speed I prefer, and I can get agitated. I can get snippy. I can get mean. I bark out orders. I assign tasks at the speed of light. My family wants to revolt every time. I am trying to become less anxious, worried, obsessed, indignant, fussy, troubled, and worked up so that I do not fall into the Martha trap.

Read the following verses and summarize them in your own words:

Isaiah 35:3-4

1 Peter 5:7

Psalm 94:19

John 14:27

When was the last time you felt anxious? What was it about? In retrospect, was it as scary or important or dangerous as you thought?

To which of the three adjectives—distracted, anxious, isolated—can you most relate? Why?

When are you most likely to fall into the "Martha trap" and concern yourself with the wrong things?

Anxiety is a common theme in Scripture because it is a common problem. For Martha. For me. For you. I think we can all easily fall into the Martha trap—maybe not about our hospitality, but maybe about our possessions, our families, our titles, our security, our policies, our power, and our relationships.

The solution to distraction, anxiety, and isolation is to lean into your relationship with God. In His presence and focused on Him, you can stop and remember how big God is and how much He loves you. When you're most tempted to withdraw from God or feel like you can't take the time away to be with Him, that is the time when you need to lean into Him the most. When you do, you'll find your relationships with others improving as well.

Call to Action

Choose one or more of the following:

- Sometimes, our attitude can be improved by practicing gratitude. Send a card of thanks to a few people who dedicate their lives to helping others: soldiers, police officers, teachers, firefighters, and medical staff, to name a few.
- Sometimes our possessions can distract us, especially if they become clutter without usefulness or purpose. Start a box of donations to give to a charity.
- Paint inspirational words and sayings on rocks and place them throughout your community. Include messages about letting go of worry and trusting God.
- Pray that God would help you in your feelings of isolation, anxiety, and distraction to feel His presence and practice reaching out to others.

Weekly Wrap-up

One evening many years ago, Scott and I were going to visit some new friends. We had never been to their house and we were looking forward to a great night together. We rang the doorbell and without much of a pause, a loud noise came from the other side of the door. Their dog, which we guessed was a Mastiff, Great Dane, or California grizzly bear, caused us to take a few additional steps back, protect our extremities, and hide our valuables.

However, when they opened the door, we laughed. Their dog, much to our surprise, was quite small. It was standing in a long, cavernous hallway—a perfect place for optimum acoustics. It was a shock. And a good reminder that things are not always what they seem.

We know a lot about Martha, Mary, and Lazarus. But there is much we do not know as well. We know they had a friendship with Jesus and were supporters of His ministry. We know they spent time with Him. We know the story of Lazarus's raising from the dead and how many came to faith because of it.

However, just like the dog in the long hallway, we do not see the whole picture. Did they get along? Did they have a true sibling rivalry? Did they always support one another in their separate ministries? Those questions remain unanswered.

One thing is certain: They all had valuable parts to play in the story of God. Listening to God, making Jesus our focus, embracing change in others, dropping the labels we give others, rejoicing in the ministry of others, and avoiding the pitfalls of service are some of the many lessons we can glean from the examples of Martha, Mary, and Lazarus—both good and bad.

Some of the most influential and godly people I know struggle to see their value in the larger story of God. Though I do not have the ability to see the big picture of anyone's life, here are a few things I do know to be true: (1) God made each of us to make a difference; (2) God fearfully and wonderfully made you and me, and sometimes the things He asks of us stir in us a mixture of fear and wonder; and (3) We were created to do good works in response to the perfect work that Jesus did on the cross for each of us.

Do you struggle to believe how much God loves *you*? Do you wonder how He wants to use you to draw people to Himself and where you fit in His story? The Bible holds the answers. It is not just a book of wisdom; it provides hard data of God's love, faithfulness, and desire to write you into the greatest love story ever told!

Group Session Guide:
WEEK 3

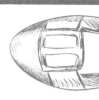

Mary, Martha, and Lazarus

Appreciating the Contributions of Others

> Each of us has a unique relationship with Jesus, and we can all benefit from the gifts and experiences that others share with us.

Welcome/Prayer/Icebreaker (5–10 minutes)

Welcome to Session 3 of *Common Ground: Loving Others Despite Our Differences*. This week we've explored the lives of Mary, Martha, and Lazarus—siblings who related to Jesus in unique but equally important ways. Today we will discover how these siblings' lives parallel our own.

Take a moment to open with prayer, and then invite each woman to name and share how a unique contribution of one family member has enriched her life personally. Point out how our families can bring out the best as well as the worst of us, as this week's study highlighted.

Video (about 20 minutes)

Play the video segment for Week 3, filling in the blanks as you watch and making notes about anything that resonates with you or that you want to be sure to remember.

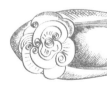

Group Session Guide:
WEEK 3

—Video Notes—

Key Scripture: Romans 12:4-5

Different _____: "One body with many members"

Celebrating others increases our: _____, _____,

_____, _____

Different _____: "These members do not all have the same function"

Same _____: "In Christ"

Same _____: "Each member belongs to all the others . . ."

Other Insights:

Group Discussion (20–25 minutes for a 60-minute session; 30–35 minutes for a 90-minute session)

Video Discussion

- Read aloud Romans 12:4-5. How do these verses relate to the topic of appreciating the contributions of others? What lessons can we learn from Mary, Martha, and Lazarus about appreciating the contributions of others?
- How does celebrating others benefit us? (*Leader notes*: It increases our strength/health, satisfaction, success, and self-control)
- Read Proverbs 11:25 (CEB). What are some ways that we can refresh others and celebrate their gifts?
- How does celebrating others change the way we see and feel about ourselves? When have you experienced this?
- Why is it important to remember that we have the same Savior and belong to one another? What does it mean to say that we belong to one another?

Group Session Guide: WEEK 3

Workbook Discussion

- Do you relate more to Mary or Martha right now? Why? (Day 1, page 83)
- How is Jesus trying to get your attention—or how has He gotten your attention in the past? (Day 1, page 83)
- Who in your life keeps Jesus as the center of attention, from your vantage point? (Day 2, page 88)

- Have you ever been given a negative label by others—or yourself? Loser? Disappointment? Not good enough? Irrelevant? How did you feel when receiving that label? (Day 4, page 97)
- Have you ever labeled others because of their flaws and then "trapped" them there without giving them space to grow? Explain. (Day 4, page 98)

- Has anyone ever called out your unique, positive, God-given qualities? What was that experience like?
- In your sphere of influence, who needs to be reminded of their value as God's beloved child?

- What in your life is taking your eyes off the most important priorities? (Day 5, page 102)
- To which of the three adjectives—distracted, anxious, isolated—can you most relate? Why? (Day 5, page 105)

- What happens in your life when you take your focus off of Jesus and put it on secondary things?

Connection Point (10–15 minutes—90-minute session only)

Divide into groups of two to three and discuss the following:

- According to Ephesians 1:13-14, what kind of mark does God place on you when you become a believer? (Day 4, page 98)
- What hinders you from giving yourself time to sit with Jesus and hear Him speak to you?

- What steps can you take to be more receptive and open toward Jesus?

Closing Prayer (5 minutes)

Close the session by sharing personal prayer requests and praying for one another. If you like, invite the women to surround those who have shared requests and pray for them aloud. In addition to praying aloud for one another, close by asking God to help you appreciate and celebrate the contribution of others.

Week 4

Rachel and Leah

Having Compassion for the Plight of Others

Memory Verse

Do nothing out of selfish ambition or vain conceit. Rather, in humility value others above yourselves.
(Philippians 2:3)

Biblical Background

Did you know that Adidas and Puma companies were the result of a rivalry between siblings? The two athletic shoe empires were started by two men from the same family. German brothers Adolf and Rudolf Dassler created a shoe company in the 1920s in the laundry room of their mother's house. As the business grew, so did the antagonism between the two men. The Second World War actually created an insurmountable rift between the two entrepreneurs. Adolf started Adidas, and Rudolf created Puma; and the sibling rivalry played out in the athletic shoe industry.[1]

Another sibling rivalry between two brothers that may be more familiar is that of Jacob and Esau. The irony of the story of Jacob is that this man whose name means "deceiver" and who famously tricked his brother is later bamboozled himself by his uncle and future father-in-law (more about that later). Through deception, Jacob stole not only the birthright but also the blessing due to his elder brother. First, he tricked Esau into selling his birthright for a bowl of stew. Later, with the help of his mother, he went to his father, Isaac—who sat in darkness with failing eyesight—and used his father's blindness, goatskins, and a good meal (never underestimate the power of a good burger) to deceive the patriarch and take his brother's blessing.

Jacob fled from the wrath of his brother, the coddling of his mother, and the loss of his father. His trip took him over five hundred miles to Paddan Aram, the land of his mother and the home of his Uncle Laban. When Jacob arrived, he took one look at Rachel, his uncle's daughter, and fell in love. He worked seven years for her hand in marriage, and when the time came for them to be joined, Laban deceived Jacob. Using the tool of darkness, Laban sent his eldest daughter, Leah (Rachel's sister), into the tent to consummate the marriage. (Jacob would agree to work another seven years to have Rachel as his wife, also.) It's noteworthy that sight and darkness played a role in both Jacob's and Laban's deceptions.

Another recurring theme in the story of Jacob's family is infertility. In Genesis 25:21, we find that his mother, Rebekah, was childless and seemingly unable to conceive without divine intervention. And divine intervention is what she got! In the same verse, we see that God answered the prayer of her husband, Isaac, and blessed them with twin sons. One of those twins, Jacob, grew up to marry a woman with fertility issues of her own—his beloved Rachel.

The story of Rachel and Leah gives us the opportunity to see how two sisters from the same family handled heartache. The struggles they faced could have been common ground for a deeper relationship between them, but instead, they allowed rivalry and jealousy to tear them apart. It's a sad story, because we sisters (biological or not) need one another!

Day 1: May the Odds Be Ever in Your Favor

Scripture Focus

Genesis 29:1-20

Today's Key Verses

¹⁶Now Laban had two daughters; the name of the older was Leah, and the name of the younger was Rachel. ¹⁷Leah had weak eyes, but Rachel had a lovely figure and was beautiful.

(*Genesis 29:16-17*)

When our daughter, Judah, entered high school, my husband and I prayed for her like crazy. I am not sure who was more nervous, Judah or us. We were new to the town, and she had not had time to make any friends yet—a hard way to start high school. To make matters worse, she had only attended private school up to this point. At her private school, all the students knew one another, the teachers truly cared for each child, class sizes were small, and I was on staff—so there was always the added element of security. At her new school, she knew no one.

God answered some of our prayers in the first week. She met a few girls who made her feel more comfortable, but one in particular gave us great hope. Judah and this young lady clicked right away. Although they were very different in appearance, in their interests, and in their academic goals, the girls became a great source of encouragement for each other. They both loved Jesus, and that seemed to be enough.

Before I go any farther, I have to say that I think my daughter is extraordinary. She has beautiful brown eyes that engage and sparkle and complement her brown locks. She is strong, smart, and fun to be around. She is fiercely protective of her friends and family. She can act the stuffing out of any script, and she has the voice of an angel. She is truly beautiful inside and out.

But the covers of magazines are not filled with photos of celebrities that look like my daughter. (They should be, but they are not.) She is very bright and creative, but academics are not something about which she is passionate. Judah was always more concerned about loving others and doing well in performances than earning a shining grade on her report card. Judah encourages those around her, gives spectacular hugs, sets a great example for her brother, and is wise beyond her years, but those qualities do not show up on an SAT or ACT score.

Her new friend, on the other hand, was a blonde-haired, blue-eyed beauty. She always excelled in sports, in academics, and in attracting a long line of boys who wanted to date her. With Judah's encouragement, she began acting and singing and soon got leading roles and solos.

The girls really cheered each other on, but this season was not easy for our girl. Judah cared for her new friend and encouraged her, but our daughter must have fallen into the "compare snare" once or twice (or a zillion times) in the four years of high school.

I fell into it myself. I grew to really love this young lady and her mom, but there were days that the feelings of unfairness crept into my shallow heart. The odds and advantages seemed to be stacked in this other girl's favor.

The relationship between Judah and her friend reminds me of the story of Rachel and Leah. Before we meet these two sisters, let's set the stage. In Genesis 27, Jacob stole Esau's blessing by pretending to be Esau. When Esau found out, he vowed to kill Jacob. Jacob's mother, Rebekah, heard what Esau said, so she sent Jacob to her brother Laban in Harran. Genesis 28 gives us an account of Jacob traveling to Harran (and the famous dream of the ladder from heaven). Let's pick up the story in the next chapter.

Read Genesis 29:1-14.

How did Jacob discover that he had reached his uncle's lands?

How did Jacob meet Rachel?

How did Jacob respond when he met her?

When Rachel discovered that Jacob was a relative, how did she respond?

How was Jacob received by Laban?

Everything seems to be working in Jacob's favor. He arrived in the open country and met shepherds from Harran, where Laban lived. Then he met Rachel, Laban's daughter and a shepherdess who had come to water her father's flock. Jacob kissed Rachel and wept aloud at finding his relatives. Rachel told Laban about Jacob, and Laban brought Jacob home and accepted him as a part of the family. Then comes the first plot twist in a saga fitting for prime-time TV.

Read Genesis 29:15-20.

What question did Laban ask Jacob?

What was Jacob's response?

What do we discover about Laban's daughters?

What arrangement did Jacob and Laban make?

When we meet Rachel and Leah, the odds seem to be stacked in the favor of the younger sister for sure. "Now Laban had two daughters; the name of the older was Leah, and the name of the younger was Rachel. Leah had weak eyes, but Rachel had a lovely figure and was beautiful" (vv. 16-17).

Let's start with their names. With a name like Amberly, I certainly cannot judge, but Leah's name means "wearied," "dull," "stupid," "pining" or "yearning."[2] Holy labels, Batman! That is a brutal list and not an inaccurate foreshadowing. Yikes.

The name of the younger was Rachel, which means "ewe," a female sheep. Although I cannot imagine that being named after a farm animal is anything short of therapy-inducing, it was a compliment in that culture. In a society where shepherding was the main source of income, such a name would have honored the bearer. We don't name our kids after farm animals, but maybe we should. "C'mon, Bovine, wash up for dinner!" "Hey, Colt, have you finished your home-work?" "Heifer, Steer, and Ox, don't make me pull this car over..."

> **What does your name mean? Write it below, along with its meaning. If you don't know the meaning, look it up on the internet.**

Next comes the topic of looks. Leah was described as having "weak eyes." Some Bible commentators think that her eyes were weak or unfit for the dusty land on which she lived.[3] Other scholars think she might have had soft, blue eyes, which was seen (no pun intended) as an imperfection at that time.[4] That one feature is all that was mentioned about Leah.

On the other hand, Rachel had more adjectives used to describe her than Tolkien used to describe the Shire. "Rachel was beautiful and well-favored" (v. 17, ASV). That was one way of saying *Wowza*. On a scale from one to ten, she was a 17.5!" She had a great figure and a beautiful face—the combo platter of awesome. How unfair does that seem?

As if that was not enough, the first time Jacob laid eyes on Rachel, she had sheep with her—an indicator that she came from a family with means. It was the modern-day equivalent of driving up in a Porsche! So, add wealth to beauty and a good figure. That just seems like a perfect recipe for love at first sight. No wonder Jacob was willing to work seven years for Rachel!

Sometimes when we see the advantages or blessings of others, we forget how blessed we are. Let's take a few moments to assess for ourselves how fair things seem for us.

Below, is a list of attributes and a line indicating a spectrum for each. On each line, place a mark where you believe you land.

Looks:

Ugly   **Supermodel Gorgeous**

_____

Education:

Never educated   **Doctorate degree**

_____

Finances:

Penniless   **Rich**

_____

Physical Health:

Sick frequently   **Rarely Sick**

_____

Spiritual Health:

Never heard the gospel   **Growing follower of Jesus**

_____

We use our limited human eyes when we judge fairness, but in doing so, we forget that God's perspective is so much greater. Let's revisit the categories we evaluated. My hope is that in doing so, we will recognize just how blessed we are.

- **Looks**. According to a recent global survey by the Dove corporation, a company that manufactures beauty products, only four out of a hundred women consider themselves beautiful. However, 80 percent of women believe that *every* woman has something beautiful about her. If you do not know how truly beautiful you are, you are not alone.[5] And you are not alone if you feel less than others in the looks department.

- **Education**. "UIS data shows that 750 million adults, two-thirds of which are women, still lack basic reading and writing skills."[6] If you have not-so-pleasant memories about number two pencils, mean teachers, or the Pythagorean theorem, or if you know the joy of getting lost in a good book, you have an advantage over millions of people in the world.

- **Finances**. According to statistics from recent years, more than 650 million people live on less than $1.90 a day.[7] If you have more than $1.50 in change in your car console, under the cushions of your couch, or in your wallet, you have an unfair advantage over more people than approximately double the population of the United States.

- **Physical Health**. In 2015, 29 percent of the world's population still did not have access to clean water.[8] Regardless of the current state of your health, if you have clean water to make tea, coffee, or a frappuccino, you have an advantage over more than 25 percent of the world's population when it comes to a basic necessity for good health.

- **Spiritual Health**. If you have a Bible, if you have a relationship with Jesus, and if someone has shared Jesus with you, you are blessed indeed. There are still an estimated 7,400 people groups who are considered unreached. That means over 42 percent of the world's population hasn't heard about Jesus.[9]

The truth is, you and I are abundantly blessed. When we look at these statistics, we recognize we have an unfair advantage over most of the world. We are the Rachels. Have you ever considered that? You and I are advantaged. If we fail to see that, we can get stuck in self-pity.

Besides the areas we have discussed thus far, what are some other ways you and I are advantaged? Make a list below:

Do you believe there are any advantages to self-pity? Explain.

If there are no advantages to self-pity, why do you think many of us struggle with it?

Once we acknowledge how blessed and privileged we are, we should strive to use those blessings for the glory of God.

How can you leverage your advantages to help other people?

How can you use your advantages to point others to Jesus?

As we pause our study of Jacob, Leah, and Rachel for today, let's reflect on how blessed we are and how we can use our resources to bless others who may not have the same opportunities and advantages.

When I encounter statistics and situations that make me realize just how blessed I am, I am humbled. I have a safe place to live, a family I love, a job I enjoy, a group of friends with whom I connect, and plenty of clothes to wear. (I am reminded of this final blessing every time I have to do laundry!) But gratitude for these possessions is not enough. If I want to find common ground with others, I must put my gratitude into action and leverage the things I have to help those who have less. Won't you join me?

Call to Action

Choose one or more of the following:

- Use your blessings to organize a community project or church event.
- Write generic letters of encouragement to those who are disadvantaged or discouraged. Take them to your church and ask your pastor or ministry leader to distribute them. Or you could ask them to give you names and addresses of people so you can mail them directly.

- Gather items for those who are homeless—food, water, toiletries, grocery gift cards, socks (the homeless population's most requested item!).[10] and notes of encouragement. Keep these items in your car and give them to the next homeless person you see. Smile at him or her when you bless a person with the package.
- Pray that God would heighten your awareness of new things (and people) for which to be thankful.

Day 2: Taking the Wheel

Scripture Focus

Genesis 29:20–30:1-24

Today's Key Verses

[1]*When Rachel saw that she was not bearing Jacob any children, she became jealous of her sister. So she said to Jacob, "Give me children, or I'll die!"*

[2]*Jacob became angry with her and said, "Am I in the place of God, who has kept you from having children?"*

(Genesis 30:1-2)

When I was in high school, I dated a young man for a few years. He and I met at a party, and his smile was the first thing I noticed about him. After an hour or so of chitchat, he started talking about his pride and joy—his car. I do not think about cars much, except when they break down, but I listened intently to his ramblings about the motor, the difficulties of reupholstering, and the numerous hours he had spent underneath the hood making it a driving machine. It was clearly an obsession for him.

When he came to pick me up for our first date, I was shocked. While he had gone into such painstaking detail about his car, he never mentioned make or model. I assumed it was either a classic or a sports car of sorts. Again, I don't care much about vehicles, but when he pulled up, I almost laughed aloud.

It was a Chevy Citation X-11. Before you go researching that make and model in *Car and Driver*, just know it was not a classic. It was classically ugly. My date's Citation was clean, meticulously detailed with racing stripes (oh, the irony!), and a source of great pride for my date. I am not trying to be unkind, but the car did not live up to the hype.

I remember the day he got new seats for his car. When they came in, he was so excited that he called me so I could hear the package open. I offered to help install them (with my major lack of mechanical knowledge). When my mom dropped me off, my car guy met me with a huge grin and a toolbox of gadgets I knew nothing about. But I was a willing extra set of hands to tackle the removal of the old and the installation of the new.

It took much longer than we had anticipated to install them—hours longer. We had grown hungry and grumpy, and we needed lunch. But how would we get to a store or restaurant to buy food? I offered to walk, but my boyfriend had a different idea. He placed plastic outdoor chairs in the space where the old seat covers were housed. We knew it was not legal, but we chose to take a chance anyway; it was only two miles or so, and we could take back streets most of the way. We rode to the store in chairs designed for BBQs and lounging—certainly not for driving around in a Chevy.

We made it to the store safely (by the grace of God), bought lunch, and headed back to his house to finish the installation. About two blocks from his home, he turned a corner too abruptly, lost his balance in the car, and fell backward. What happened next can only be recalled in my mind in slow motion. On his journey backward, he let go of the steering wheel and yelled. I looked back to check on him but failed to grab the steering wheel in time. We crashed into a parked car and, despite the fact that we were not going very fast, both cars were pretty mangled. Fortunately, we were unharmed and there was no one in the other vehicle, but his precious baby was totaled.

Our relationship did not last much past that day, but the lesson sure did. Not only the "don't drive sitting in lawn furniture" lesson, but also one that reminds me of our theme for today—taking the wheel of control from God.

In the story of Rachel and Leah, people manipulated others and circumstances to get what they wanted. They would not wait on God's timing and provision (not unlike two teens wanting lunch), so they exploited, controlled, influenced, orchestrated, and steered the outcome the way they wanted. I am sure you have *never* done that—at least not today. Right?

Read Genesis 29:20-30.

How long did Jacob work for Laban in exchange for Rachel's hand in marriage?

What does the Scripture say about those years?

How did Laban and the family celebrate the wedding?

What did Laban do to deceive Jacob? What excuse did Laban give for doing so?

How do you think you would feel if you had been Leah?

What does verse 30 tell you about the relationships in this passage?

Laban, the father of Rachel and Leah, was a shrewd businessman. When Jacob offered to work for seven years in order to marry Rachel, the greedy Laban accepted. According to some scholars, the average payment for a bride (women were considered property at the time), was the equivalent of a few years of labor. Jacob was willing to work twice as long as the cultural norm.[11] That's how much he wanted to marry Rachel. If Laban had a ringtone on his phone, I think it would sound like the *Jaws* theme. Just sayin'. He knew Jacob was easy prey.

The worst of Laban's behavior occurred once the seven years of labor had been satisfied. He deceived Jacob into marrying and sleeping with Leah instead of Rachel, his love (Genesis 29:23). Now before we start getting righteously indignant for our guy, Jacob, we need to remember a few things. Jacob deceived his brother out of his birthright for some stew, and he stole the blessing reserved for his brother by leveraging his father's poor eyesight. Jacob was not a blameless dude.

Jacob was essentially deceived using the same tactics he had employed. Jacob used the darkness of his father's eyesight to fool him (Isaac). Laban used the darkness of night and manipulated the situation to get seven more years of labor from Jacob. Laban did not take responsibility for his deception. He blamed it on custom. Jacob had used custom and tradition to get what he wanted too.

We have all done things to get what we want. Babies cry to get milk or a fresh diaper. Teenagers rebel to get the attention of parents. Employees embellish résumés to get a new job. Singles fill their profiles with a picture of someone either younger, or more attractive, or both. People cut corners to save money on taxes. I'm not trying to stereotype anyone. I'm saying that *all of us* have been guilty of trying to manipulate the situation when things are not going our way. When that happens, we are taking the wheel of control out of the hands of the Almighty. And that never ends well.

Read Genesis 29:31; 30:1-12, 17-24.

Why was Rachel jealous of Leah?

Write the exchange between Rachel and Jacob in your own words:

In the space provided, write the names of the children born to the women mentioned in the passage.

Leah	Zilpah (Leah's servant)	Rachel	Bilhah (Rachel's servant)

Rachel was desperate to have a child (a woman's fertility was her value in those days), so she manipulated the situation by offering Jacob her servant, Bilhah, to conceive a child with. When my husband, Scott, and I struggled with infertility, we tried numerous methods and read a zillion books on the subject. Although I never thought to give Scott my servant (which I didn't have), I got pretty desperate. It is easy to judge Rachel, but walking a mile in her infertile moccasins makes me think twice before taking a Judgy McJudgerton perspective.

Not to be outdone, when Leah stopped having children, she gave her servant Zilpah to Jacob as a means to produce more (Genesis 30:9-13).

And then there is the topic of mandrakes, a fruit found in the Middle East. In Genesis 30:14-16, Reuben, one of Leah's sons, went out and gleaned the mandrakes. The two sisters make a deal over them; Rachel wanted them because the plant was supposed to make barren women fruitful.[12] Leah gave them to her in hopes that she (Leah) could gain her husband's affection, at least for one night. It turned out to be a good trade for Leah. God heard her prayers (v. 17) and she bore Jacob a fifth son, Issachar. I guess that put the "man" in mandrake. Later this week, we will talk more about Leah and Rachel and their competition. For now, remember that both women manipulated the situation to get what they wanted.

And the manipulation and deception continued in this family's history. We don't have space to unpack those stories, but here's a quick summary.

- Jacob wanted to return to his homeland, but Laban convinced Jacob to stay because God had blessed Jacob and Laban wanted in on the blessings. (Genesis 30:25-28)
- Jacob deceived Laban to get more goats (wealth). (Genesis 30:29-43)
- When Jacob took his wives and wealth back to his homeland, Rachel stole her father's household gods on the way out. (Genesis 31:19)
- Jacob deceived Laban by not telling Laban that he and his wives were running away. (Genesis 31:20)
- Rachel lied to her father about taking the household gods (and lied about other things, too). (Genesis 31:34-35)

Have I ever tricked anyone into working for me for fourteen years? Traded mandrakes for a night of passion? Given away my servant so I could bear children? Dabbled in animal husbandry? No. But I've done my share of manipulation and deception to get what I wanted.

I have had seasons when I thought my ways and my desires were better than God's. Times when, if I was honest, I thought my clock and time line were more accurate than God's. Times when I was certain that my plans were grander and better than the One who created Hawaii and peaches and Vanilla Swiss Almond Häagen-Dazs ice cream. (Well, "the land of milk and honey" is a good start for ice cream.)

Have you ever tried to manipulate a situation or take matters into your own hands because you grew impatient with God's timing or plans? What happened?

Are you doing that now? Explain.

Is there an area of your life you've tried to control? Do you need to hand the wheel back to God (hand control back over to Him)? Explain.

Make a list of the things that the Lord has done for you in the last three months. Was any of those an answer to prayer? Was it answered on your schedule? Explain.

Take a few moments and pray that God would heighten your awareness of areas you are trying to control and ask for His forgiveness. Remind yourself of God's faithfulness in your life and the lives of others. Write those experiences below so you can remember them when you're tempted to manipulate your situation or try to manipulate God.

I love watching kids try to "control" the car on amusement car rides. They spin the steering wheel around a million times and, yet, they have no real bearing on where the car goes. The ride does what it has been programmed and designed to do, but kids still wear themselves out trying.

There are times when I fool myself into thinking that I can take the steering wheel from the Lord of the Universe and manipulate and control things until I get what I want. I make plans without consulting God, I follow my dreams without asking about His dreams for me, and even worse, sometimes I go my own way. When I do that, I am no different than the toddler who screams (and screams and screams) in the middle of a store because she did not get what she wanted. I just wear myself out trying.

In what areas do you struggle to relinquish control to God? Are you tired yet?

At a women's retreat I spoke about birds and two different types of flight: soaring and flapping. Eagles and like birds that soar can travel hundreds of miles without flapping their wings. The shape of their wings and the physics of the wind create an aerodynamic coupling. Smaller birds, in comparison, spend most of their time flapping their wings, relying less on the wind and more on their own abilities.

At the end of the session, one of the ladies came to me and said, "I know I am supposed to soar on wings like eagles and trust God, but instead, I am just so flappin' tired!"

If we relinquish control to God and put our hope and trust in Him, we can soar instead of wear ourselves out from flapping. There is great freedom in handing our burdens, concerns, and controls over to the One who made us. He will always work in our best interest, enabling us to soar!

Call to Action

Choose one or more of the following:

- One way to relinquish control is to focus on God's Word. Meditate on Isaiah 55:10-11.
- Relinquish control in traffic. Let another car merge in front of you. Drive in the slow lane for a while. Patiently let pedestrians cross the street.
- Hold the either the door or elevator, or both for others at every opportunity.
- Pray for God to show you areas of your life where you are trying to do things in your own strength instead of relying upon Him.

Day 3: The Cycle of More/More-itis

Scripture Focus

Genesis 29:29-34; 30:20-24

Today's Key Verse

[Fix] our eyes on Jesus, the pioneer and perfecter of faith. For the joy set before him he endured the cross, scorning its shame, and sat down at the right hand of the throne of God.

(Hebrews 12:2)

I love to shop at thrift stores. Adore it. I love the thrill of a bargain, the smell of old books, and the feeling of going on an adventure (cue "Indiana Jones" theme music). As the great theologians Deep Purple once sang, "It's not the kill, it's the thrill of the chase."[13] I love digging through boxes with a heart full of hope and a hand full of dollar bills.

Oftentimes, when I am speaking at women's retreats, I have part of the afternoon on Saturdays to rest and do as I please. I think my husband has grown weary of what this freedom can become; I have brought home a menagerie of treasures. Once, I drove three hundred miles with a piece of furniture strapped in with only bungee cords and prayer (it was only three inches too long to fit in the backseat of the rental). I spent three hundred miles listening to the car signal warning me that "the door was ajar." It was harrowing, but it was worth it!

One of my favorite "treasures" to hunt is secondhand jewelry. Some of my favorite pieces have come from garage sales, estate sales, pawn shops, and eBay. I love when I can learn the history of a piece of jewelry.

One year at Christmas, one of my students brought a small gift box to me at school. The parents of all my students were always generous, but this looked like a box that might hold jewelry, so I was extra stoked to open it. The note on the outside read: "Please do not open until you are home."

Have I mentioned that I hate waiting? I could not wait for the clock to strike 3:00 p.m. so that I could open this little box.

When I opened it, I indeed saw a piece of jewelry inside: a blue stone with what looked to be silver metal surrounding little cubic zirconia stones—or what we call "canardlies"—stones so small you "can hardly" see them. It was a pretty ring—nothing terribly fancy, but a sweet token from a family I had come to love.

The ring, however, was too small for my sausage-like fingers (story of my life). When I took it to be sized and showed it to the jeweler, he got so excited. He explained that it was a blue topaz having a cut used in the 1920s. He went on to add that what I thought were cubic zirconia stones were indeed diamonds, and that the silver metal was platinum. It was going to cost me a pretty penny to have platinum added to this delicate ring. He appraised the ring at more than I made in a month as a teacher.

I asked the jeweler not to size the ring because I needed to return it to the family that had given it to me. When I saw the matriarch of the clan the following Monday, I told her what the jeweler had said. I also explained that I could not accept a gift of such value.

She smiled. Her boys, all of whom had been in my class at one time or another, had seen this ring at an estate sale, thought I would love it, and asked if they could buy it for me. When they took it to the counter at the estate sale, the cuteness of the boys and the humble appearance of the ring allowed them to purchase the ring for a song.

The mother went on to tell me that she knew the ring was something special, but that the estate sale was run by someone who had labeled it as a trinket only.

She convinced me to take it by explaining that her boys had grown so much in my class because I had seen something special in each of them. I saw each of them as more than a trinket; I viewed them as treasures in Christ. She believes it was my view of them that gave them the tools they needed to navigate the pressures, harsh words, and labels often encountered in the junior high years.

Rachel understood the power of words and labels. Even though she was loved by Jacob, she felt great societal pressure to bear sons for him; yet she lived in heartache every twenty-eight days. She let the words of her culture give her a label, and she let it echo in her life: *barren*. But as we've already seen, the label didn't last forever.

Read Genesis 30:22-24.

What happened in these verses?

What did Rachel name the child, and what did the name mean? (v. 24)

Rachel didn't choose a name that means "Thank you, God!" or "What a relief!" or "Wow! Labor is no fun!" or "How has my sister done this seven times?" Rachel named him Joseph, which means "may the Lord add to me another son." Even when God listened to and answered her prayers for a son and she could silence the echoes in her head, she was not satisfied. Instead of finally being content, her heart was filled with dissatisfaction. She wanted another son.

Talk about a knock upside the head from Scripture. You and I are guilty of the same mistake. We lack contentment.

You move into a new house, and then you notice a newer, bigger house down the street.

You have enough food on your table, but you are jealous when a family gets to go out to eat more often than yours.

You marry the man of your dreams and then watch dreamy dudes on TV.

You get a new car but then drool when the latest model comes out.

You buy a new blouse and then grow tired of it after you wear it a few times, so you go shopping for another one.

Can you relate? I can! We live in a culture that bombards us with the "necessity" of having the latest and newest. From cars to our cell phones, we've been convinced that we *need* those things because they will make our lives better. And they do—until the next newest version hits the market. Then our contentment goes out the window.

Leah also lived with discontentment. Not the desire to have more children or a car or a cell phone, but the desire for her husband's affection.

> **Read Genesis 29:29-34. In the space below, write down how Leah named each child and what each name meant.**

Wow. Talk about pain. With each new child, she hoped she would *finally* have the attention and affection of Jacob.

If only. The Scarecrow from *The Wizard of Oz* thought his problems would be solved if only he had a brain. Our "if only" looks different:

If only I had a spouse.
If only I had a house.
If only I had a child.
If only I had obedient children.
If only I had a friend.
If only I had a bigger house.
If only I had a good job.
If only I had a pair of jeans that fit.
If only I had the right education.
If only I had plastic surgery.
If only I had a good boss.

The problem is this: Often, when we finally get what we think we want, our desires change. We start saying, "If only I had a better . . ." And the cycle of "more" begins.

> **Make a list of something you wanted at the ages listed:**
>
> **7 years old:**
>
> **16 years old:**
>
> **22 years old:**

30 years old:

45 years old:

60 years old:

Today:

How have your desires changed over time?

The good news is that the discontentment and desire for more doesn't have to be a permanent state of mind. We don't have to live in a continual cycle of discontent. We can learn a lesson from Leah.

Read Genesis 29:35. What did she name this son? What does that name mean?

With her fourth son, we can see her change of heart, at least temporarily. She took her focus off of her discontentment and put it on the satisfying goodness of God. It's a lesson you and I need to learn too.

Read Hebrews 12:2 and summarize it below.

I think this verse contains the key to stopping the "if only" voice when it starts yammering on and on in our heads. If we stop letting the echoes and labels of others define us and, instead, start focusing on who God is and what He says about us, we can break the cycle of discontentment. Though Leah did not focus on God perfectly all the time, we still can learn from her example.

For the record, you and I were created by the Master Jeweler who sees us for the treasured gems we are! Boom! We were made for a beautiful purpose and have been given great value by God's Son, Jesus Christ.

Read Ephesians 2:10. How does this verse help us break the cycle of needing more?

Ephesians 2:10 reminds us, "We are God's handiwork, created in Christ Jesus to do good works, which God prepared in advance for us to do." We are the work of His hands. That is a wonderful truth to stand on when we find ourselves in the cycle of more. We don't have to chase after possessions, titles, or affirmation to define us. We can be content because God has already given us a label. He calls us His handiwork.

Recently I read *The Clutter-Free Home* by my author friend Kathi Lipp. In the book she gave me a bloody nose with this brilliant concept. She asserts that when we hold on to things and refuse to let go, we are saying that God cannot be trusted to provide for us if we need those things in the future.[14]

The cycle of more reveals a lack of trust in God. Do we trust that God knows best? Do we trust that He is good? Do we trust that He loves us enough to always do what is best for us? Do we trust that if we do not get _____ (whatever we think we need) then there is a reason? Do we believe that God isn't trying to torture our hearts?

If you struggle with this, you are not alone. I am right there with you, sister! I often struggle with the cycle of more and say to myself, "I would be happy if _____."

Jacob wanted his brother's blessing and inheritance.

Laban wanted a laborer to work his land.

Leah wanted her husband's affection.

Rachel wanted children.

I used to think that having more would satisfy. It doesn't. It's like salty food—it leaves you thirsty. Unless you lean into the Lord. Unless you choose to be thankful and content. Unless you drop the cycle of more for the peace of knowing you have enough.

Summarize the following verses in your own words.

Psalm 16:11

Psalm 17:15

Isaiah 58:11

Philippians 4:11-12

Hebrews 13:5

In what areas do you lack contentment?

Brainstorm some actions that could grow your contentment and write them in the space provided.

If we are going to find common ground with those around us, we must first start by reminding ourselves that God can be trusted. We must be thankful for the things He has done. We need to learn to be content in all circumstances, recognizing that He is the only "more" we truly need. Only then can we shake off the jealousy and envy and competition that divide us and find unity on common ground.

Call to Action

Choose one or more of the following:

- Read a book about contentment.
- Make a list of your most valuable personal possessions. Take time to thank God for each of them.
- Cut out or print off comic strips, magazine articles, recipes, and other materials that remind you of someone. Send them the clippings and tell them how important they are to you and to God.
- A cure for discontent is to spend time serving others. Find a way to serve someone.
- Pray for God to help you recall hard data from your life and the lives of others to build your "trust fund" with Him.

Day 4: Corrosive Competition

Today's Key Verse

A heart at peace gives life to the body,
but envy rots the bones.
(Proverbs 14:30)

Scripture Focus

Genesis 29:31-35; 30:1-10

Sometimes, the stories we hear about sibling rivalries in history sound more like reality television than actual reality television does. A few shocking rivalries between sisters can be found in our history books, but they play out more like a modern drama. My sister and I only fought over clothing and who got to sit in the front seat, but sisters Mary and Anne Boleyn fought for the affection of King Henry VIII. The British monarch first took Mary as his mistress. However, the fickle leader eventually dismissed her in order to marry her sister, Anne. Their marriage appeared to be a triumph for Anne in the sibling competition since she became queen. Sadly, however, she ultimately lost when she was beheaded by her husband for supposed infidelity and the inability to produce a male heir. Many believe he killed her so he could marry someone else.[15]

The drama is not limited to those across the pond. In American history, and now in a Broadway show, we discover the Schuyler sisters, Angelica and Eliza. Although the founding father Alexander Hamilton married the younger sister Eliza, he often matched wits and exchanged flirtatious messages with the older sibling, Angelica. Although there is no concrete evidence that Alexander and Angelica ever had an affair, biographer Ron Chernow notes that the attraction between the two of them was so strong that people assumed they were lovers.[16] It's possible that the undercurrent of competition and comparison between the sisters might have caused tension if not a deep division.

I hate stories like this. It messes with my idea of Happily Ever After. I am hopelessly romantic. I want a Disney ending for everyone. Even writing about King Henry VIII makes me want to punch the man squarely in the neck, and the idea of Alexander Hamilton with wandering eyes makes my teeth itch.

When my husband, Scott, and I met, it was not love at first sight. Well, it may have been for him, but I was too busy admiring the handiwork of God in a friend of his—really excellent work, if the truth be told. I was walking to chapel at my university. Out of the corner of my eye I saw him—my major crush. At the time, I thought he was the perfect combination. He was smart, he was handsome, he loved Jesus, and he had a mullet. In 1989, that was considered awesome, so do not judge. As Mullet Man and his friend got closer, he asked, "Hey, do you want to walk to chapel with us?" Okay, so it was not Shakespeare, but it sounded poetic to me. Inside I was saying, "*Oh my*! Mullet Man wants to walk to chapel with *me*! This is the story we will tell our grandchildren someday!" Fortunately, the outside of me just said, "Sure."

On the way to chapel, Mullet Man changed my life. He said, "This is my friend, Scott Neese." I did not know it at the time, but it was Choir Boy Haircut Man not Mullet Man, who would become my beloved husband. Although I love hearing people's love stories, I am not sure Scott loves to hear me tell other people that I had my eye on Mullet Man. My husband was technically my second choice (Actually, Mullet Man was not my first choice, but let's not get technical.) No one wants to be considered Plan B. No one likes being the second choice.

Leah was most definitely Jacob's second choice. I am not even sure she would have been Plan B. Maybe Plan Q if he was stuck on a desert island with her.

Many of my friends, both single and married, read the story of Leah and Rachel and can painfully relate to being the second choice. I think we have all felt the sting of coming up short at one time or another—at work, at home, in relationships, on social media. When we compare ourselves to others, we feel like we fail miserably.

Many of my single friends can relate to Leah, watching another woman being pursued, cherished, and adored. They look at their own lives in comparison, and questions of "Why not me?" and "When will I be chosen?" plague their thoughts while feelings of inadequacy, despondency, and resignation badger their hearts.

Unfortunately, many of my married friends can also relate to Leah. Another woman wasn't in the picture (although it was for some), but these women feel that they are in constant competition with their spouses' work, golf, hobbies, or television shows. Even though they wear wedding rings on their fingers, they are haunted by questions like "Why am I not enough?" "What did I do wrong?" and "Why doesn't he care about me as much as he cares about_____?"

From our reading of Genesis 29–30, it seems God was kind to our girl, Leah. He enabled her to have four sons, because as Genesis 29:31 tells us, "the Lord saw that Leah was unloved." Leah was rejected by her husband in the love department, so she had to deal with her unfulfilled desires to be pursued. When she compared herself to Rachel, who had Jacob's affection, she came up short. She just couldn't compete—Jacob's heart clearly belonged to Rachel.

But Leah could compete in the fertility department. We studied this yesterday, but I want to revisit it for a slight shift in emphasis.

Read Genesis 29:31-35.

How many children did Leah have in these verses?

What pieces of information are found in verse 35?

In the naming of her first three children, Leah expressed heartache at not being loved by Jacob. She had come in dead last in the romance competition. But as we learned yesterday, verse 35 tells us that Leah had a fourth son, whom she named Judah, which means, "praise." She said, "This time I will praise the Lord." That name marks a shift in Leah's heart, at least temporarily. God pursued her even if her husband Jacob failed to do so. Leah's attention turned toward God. She found her security and strength in Him.

When Scott and I had our firstborn, we had been married nine years, struggled with infertility, suffered miscarriages, cried, prayed, beseeched God, tried every wives' tale, subjected our bodies to tests, and read every book on the subject. When we discussed possible names, which we began doing *years* before our first child, we would lay in bed and share our ideas with each other. I had taught for many years, so that was an inspiration for many suggestions, but also a reason for veto. I had a few students who were, shall we say, more challenging (that's putting it mildly), so their names were scratched from our list. Also, I dated my fair share in high school, so when Scott brought up a name from the list of guys I had dated (unbeknownst to him), I would veto it because I did not want that reminder of a failed relationship.

During the time that we were thinking of names, I thought about how I love that Scott's first name is biblical—Matthew. I thought about how I like that my name is a little weird (sorry, Mom). Amberly is definitely a name off the beaten path. I was born in 1969, so I am glad my name was not Wheatgrass or something like that. And I thought about how I like the fact that my sister, Allyson, and I have names that start with the same letter in the alphabet.

I guess the one advantage of those years of infertility was the amount of time we had to think about names. We hoped for two children, so we decided to come up with two names for boys and two for girls. The boys' names were easy—Joshua, Jeremiah, James, Josiah, Jude. But when it came to "J" names for girls (because we like alliteration, I guess), we were at a standstill. The two names we came up with were Jezebel (the wicked wife of King Ahab who has become an archetype for evil women) and Jael. Now Jael is a beautiful name, but it refers to the Bible character who drove a tent spike through the head of an enemy soldier. I wasn't sure I wanted my daughter to feel the pressure to live up to that name!

But one morning I was reading Genesis 29–30 in my quiet time, and when I saw the name *Judah* and its meaning, I knew it was the name I wanted. If any name fit a baby for which we were so incredibly thankful, it would be Judah, because we praised God for this child.

I know it was a boy's name originally, but our girl wears it well.

When he grew up, Leah's Judah did not always make great choices, but his name is a constant reminder of the faithfulness of God shown to Leah.

Take another look at Genesis 29:35. What happened after Leah gave birth to Judah?

We're told that Leah stopped having children after giving birth to Judah. But you know from your reading yesterday that the story doesn't end there.

Read Genesis 30:1-6. What did Rachel do to create a family?

Producing sons for your husband was a big deal in Old Testament days. Huge. So, when Rachel couldn't give that to her husband, she offered her servant to him. Now, I wouldn't let anybody take my place in the bedroom (or any other room for that matter); but the culture was different back then, and having a child through your servant was the same as having the child yourself (except without the morning sickness or the pain of childbirth!). Weird, I know. But her plan worked, because her servant produced a son named Dan. Then, the servant gave Jacob a second son. I want you to see what Rachel said at this birth.

Read Genesis 30:7-8. What did Rachel say in verse 8?

"I have won." Holy competition, Batman! I wonder if Leah heard what Rachel had said, or if she inferred it from the name Naphtali, which means "my struggle." Whatever the reason, Leah decided she wasn't done in the baby-making department.

Read Genesis 30:9-10.

What did Leah offer to Jacob?

What do you think was behind Leah's decision to offer her servant to Jacob?

I can't prove it, but based on the rest of this chapter, it seems like Leah and Rachel were in a major competition. Up to this point, six boys had been born.

After that, six more boys were born through Rachel and Leah and their servants, along with at least one daughter (and possibly more who weren't mentioned—not fair, I know). Big families existed back then, but this love triangle took it to another level.

Who has been your competition in the past? Did it ever get out of hand, leading to envy? If so, what was the result? Journal about it in the space below.

Read Proverbs 14:30 in the margin. According to this verse, what is the result of envy?

A heart at peace gives life to the body,
But envy rots the bones.
(Proverbs 14:30)

In the saga of Rachel and Leah, Jacob's love for Rachel is undeniable, which fuels the competition and envy between the sisters. But I do not want to imply in any way that Rachel's inability to have children reflected God's displeasure with her. God's love doesn't operate like that. God did not love Rachel any less than her sister. Both women were struggling with disappointment and heartache, but it took on different forms for each woman. The pain was the common ground. Unfortunately, they couldn't get past the competition to see that they actually had a common enemy: insecurity.

If we want to find common ground with difficult people in our lives, we may need to focus on the things that connect us, even if it is heartache. These two women could have been an amazing support system for each other. Instead, they chose to compete.

List your three closest friends below and write five things you have in common with each one.

1)

2)

3)

4)

5)

Think of someone who is not your favorite person, and write below five things you have in common with that person.

1)

2)

3)

4)

5)

Finding common ground sometimes looks like discovering common interests, but other times it may look like praying for the person who shares a common pain or heartache that you both bear. And that requires you to look past the surface to see what might be really going on in that person's life. It requires compassion instead of comparison, and empathy instead of judgment.

For those of you who like Happily Ever After stories as much as I do, I want to point out that God did something truly remarkable through Leah. Although the older sister was the second choice of Jacob, God granted Leah the honor of being in the bloodline of both David and Jesus. Both men were descendants of Judah, the child for whom Leah bore and then praised God.

When things do not feel or look like a Happily Ever After story, God is still at work. When it seems that the advantages are stacked for others rather than in our favor, we must trust the plans of our heavenly Father and believe that He is working in our best interests, even when we cannot see it.

Call to Action

Choose one or more of the following:

- Make a list of political leaders in both parties. Despite their political beliefs, pray that God might reveal Himself to each person, and pray they might be able to work toward finding common ground.
- Do something kind for your coworkers or others who are part of a team or other group you are a part of in order to show how important they are to you.
- Make a list of people with whom you feel like you are competing (even if it is a friendly competition). Call and ask how you can be praying for them.
- Pray for those in your life who are struggling.

Day 5: End of Story

Today's Key Verses

[1]*Therefore if you have any encouragement from being united with Christ, if any comfort from his love, if any common sharing in the Spirit, if any tenderness and compassion,* [2]*then make my joy complete by being like-minded, having the same love, being one in spirit and of one mind.*

(Philippians 2:1-2)

Scripture Focus

Genesis 31:1-55

Thomas Jefferson and John Adams were two of America's founding fathers, and as Joseph Ellis wrote, they could be considered "the odd couple of the American Revolution."[17] They were both delegates to the Continental Congress and served as diplomats in Europe, and Adams selected Jefferson to pen the Declaration of Independence. But differing opinions on foreign policy, division between party lines, and divisive gossip soured a once sweet friendship.

Benjamin Rush, a mutual friend of both men, wrote to both of them, encouraging them to make amends. He described them as the "North and South Poles of the American Revolution."[18] This fellow signer of the Declaration of Independence suggested to each of the two feuding Founding Fathers that his rival wanted to see their friendship rekindle. He told Adams that he dreamed that the two would renew their relationship, discuss past issues, make amends, and sink "into the grave nearly at the same time, full of years and rich in the gratitude and praises of their country."[19]

Rush succeeded in starting correspondence between the two feuding men. In January 1812, Adams sent a note to Jefferson, which began fourteen years of constant correspondence and 158 letters exchanged between them. In 1813, Adams wrote: "You and I ought not to die...before we have explained ourselves to each other."[20] They served as a great support for each other in the last years of their lives.

But Rush's dream did more than spark a reconciliation—it proved to be prophetic. Jefferson and Adams died on the same day, July 4, 1826, on the fiftieth anniversary of Independence Day. Adams's last words were, "Thomas Jefferson still lives" or by another account, "Thomas Jefferson survives."[21]

We uncovered the issues that separated Jacob's wives, Rachel and Leah. We know why there was animosity between Jacob and Laban. And when we read the entire story of Jacob, we also understand the bad blood between Jacob and Esau, his brother. Jacob was a drama magnet. He would have been very successful on YouTube.

Genesis 31 contains another conflict involving Jacob.

Read Genesis 31:1-3.

Who is involved in this conflict?

What did God promise Jacob?

Jealousy reared its ugly head again, this time with Jacob's father-in-law. Jacob hadn't taken anything from Laban, but Jacob's wealth was increasing, which fueled mistrust and envy on Laban's part. As a result, God intervened and told Jacob to return to his homeland, assuring Jacob of His presence.

Can you think of a reason why Jacob would be worried about returning home? List any concerns he might have had.

Returning home meant returning to face Esau, his twin and the one who had sworn to kill him for taking his birthright and blessing. This was no small issue. Before we look at their reunion, let's return to the story at hand.

Read Genesis 31:4-16.

What did Jacob tell Leah and Rachel about their father?

Do you think they believed him? Explain.

To whom did Jacob attribute his wealth?

Compare verse 6 to verses 11-13. What new information do we discover about Jacob's dream?

What had happened at Bethel? (Refer to Genesis 28:10-15.)

What promise had God made to Jacob at Bethel?

What significant thing occurred in verses 14-16?

Jacob told Leah and Rachel about the situation with their father, and they were willing to return to his homeland with him, which was no small decision. They would be leaving their own home and their father. Perhaps Laban's behavior over the past decades had soured their relationship with him. Or perhaps it was a simple matter of money, as their father had used up their inheritance (31:15-16). What's important is that Leah and Rachel were on the same page.

For the first time since we met them in Genesis 29, Rachel and Leah were not at odds; they were on the same side. Team Betrayed is not a fun team to be on, but for these two, it created a sense of unity. They put down their boxing gloves and turned their indignation toward Laban. Both women felt disenfranchised by their father and disappointed that their inheritance (and their children's inheritance) had probably been compromised or even used up. We get a glimmer of hope that these two do not stay divided forever.

Jacob and his clan, along with all of his livestock, took off for home without telling Laban goodbye, which didn't set well with Laban. He pursued them until he caught up with them. We do not know if he wanted to keep the blessing of God (30:27), to say goodbye to his children and grandchildren, to take Jacob's possessions, or to fight Jacob. After a conversation that belongs in a soap opera, Jacob and Laban made a covenant.

Read Genesis 31:43-55.

What did Laban say belonged to him, not Jacob? What does this infer about Laban's perspective?

Define the term covenant in your own words below.

What was the purpose of their covenant?

What names did the covenant have?

What were the conditions of the covenant?

You've probably heard or seen Genesis 31:49 as a token of love in a wedding or on a romantic card: "May the LORD keep watch between you and me when we are away from each other." If you read this verse in context, you discover Laban wasn't feeling warm fuzzies when he made the statement. In fact, he was pretty ticked off and distrustful of Jacob.

Jacob and Laban didn't reconcile exactly. It was more of a truce and parting of ways. According to scholars, a heap of stones was laid in a circle and served as seats. In the middle of the circle, a large stone was set up perpendicularly as an altar. They probably offered a sacrifice first, and then they ate together.[22] The stones would be the reminder of their covenant. Laban set up the terms of the promise and Jacob agreed to them. The next morning, they said goodbye in the fashion of a Hallmark movie and went their separate ways.

On the trip home, Jacob had another reconciliation of sorts.

Read Genesis 32:22-32.

Whom did Jacob encounter?

What "gift" did the visitor give Jacob at daybreak?

In a famous wrestling match with a divine visitor, Jacob met his match. We don't know exactly who or what it was, but Jacob thought it was God: "It is because I saw God face to face, and yet my life was spared" (32:30). In this struggle, Jacob discovered he could not fall back on his self-reliance or trickery, but he still held on to his stubbornness. Jacob would not let go, so his visitor touched Jacob's hip and showed him the extent of his frail humanity. Jacob finally surrendered.

As a symbol of Jacob's new identity, the visitor gave him a new name: Israel. It comes from two Hebrew words meaning "wrestle" and "God."[23] The Israelite nation would come from the descendants of Israel's twelve sons. Hence the twelve tribes of Israel.[24]

When have you wrestled with God? What happened as a result?

I want to show you one more reconciliation. It's found in the next chapter.

Read Genesis 33:1-4. What famous reconciliation takes place in these verses?

¹Therefore if you have any encouragement from being united with Christ, if any comfort from his love, if any common sharing in the Spirit, if any tenderness and compassion, ²then make my joy complete by being like-minded, having the same love, being one in spirit and of one mind.
(Philippians 2:1-2)

Jacob had come full circle. He had run away from Esau as a deceiver and returned home a man surrendered to God. At this point, if I was Esau, I would want to sell my conniving brother on eBay. But that's not what happened. The two embraced and Esau forgave Jacob/Israel, who then settled in Sukkoth and built a home for himself and his family there.

What do you think was key in their reconciliation?

Although it is not a perfect ending for our man Jacob or for his wives, huge strides were made on four fronts: Rachel and Leah found some common ground; Jacob made a truce with Laban; Jacob surrendered to God; and Jacob and Esau, a rivalry equal to that of Hugh Jackman and Ryan Reynolds, reconciled with each other.

If we are to find common ground with one another, even those who have cheated us or those we have cheated, we need to remember that it *is* possible. By the grace of God and the blood of Jesus, it is possible.

Read Philippians 2:1-2 in the margin. According to these verses, how can we find common ground?

Because of Jesus Christ, finding common ground can be a reality, not just a pipe dream. We will not be best friends with everyone, but we can demonstrate mutual respect. We can show compassion and love to others—because Christ has shown compassion and love to us.

What are the characteristics of compassion, in your opinion?

If followers of Christ showed compassion for the plight of others, how would your community be different? How would our country be different?

In what area of your life do you need to show more compassion? (coworkers, boss, spouse, children, yourself, others)

The cultural landscape of our world would look radically different if believers led with compassion, even toward those who vote differently, worship differently, hold different worldviews, and live in different socioeconomic realities.

The common ground on the battleground is this: God loves us. All of us. Even when we are at our worst. As we accept and embrace this unconditional love, we can then offer it to others. In fact, that's the only proper response.

Call to Action

Choose one or more of the following:

- Create art around the theme of finding common ground with others.
- Extend compassion by distributing cold water bottles to mail carriers, construction workers, and garbage collectors in hot weather. Give hot chocolate to those who serve in your community in cold weather. Show compassion for the hard work they do.
- Sometimes, compassion looks like stopping at a kids' lemonade stand and buying a drink. Ask them why they are raising money. Give them a generous tip.
- Pray to find "common ground" with those in your life who are most difficult for you to love. Ask God to give you a heart for them.

Weekly Wrap-Up

The other day, we watched an old movie as a family. I found myself a little distracted by the black-and-white format of the film. It took time for me to adjust to the outdated technology, but finally I eased into it and was sucked into a wonderful story.

The story of Rachel and Leah can seem so disconnected from our lives today. It took place so long ago, and the culture was so different. The cause of their schism was unique, but the themes of their story have not changed one bit. We want what others have. We want things to be fair (in our eyes). We want control. We want peace. We want prosperity. And we get pulled apart because of those competing desires.

If we are striving for common ground, we must first reconcile with God, draw close to Him, and then encourage those around us to do the same. And, when that happens, we grow closer to one another.

This week, we watched the story of these two sisters unfold. The mothers of the twelve tribes of Israel are known most for their discord rather than their contribution to the nation of God. For most of their lives, they chose not to find common ground, and instead, they found jealousy, comparison, and dissatisfaction. Leah's sadness over the lack of affection from her husband left a void of discontentment. Rachel grew in her jealousy and desire to have a child, and she tried to take matters into her own hands.

When we face difficulties with one another, we have the choice to lean into God and His plan or turn away from Him. We can become bitter or we can find a way to work together. We can take matters into our own hands to manipulate the outcome (which never turns out like we'd imagined), or we can listen for the instructions of our Father who is working in our best interests, even when we cannot see how. The common ground on the battleground is our faith and trust in God.

Group Session Guide: WEEK 4

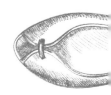

Rachel and Leah

Having Compassion
for the Plight of Others

Compassion and contentment are antidotes
to envy in today's culture of "more."

Welcome/Prayer/Icebreaker (5–10 minutes)

Welcome to Session 4 of *Common Ground: Loving Others Despite Our Differences*. This week we've explored the relationship between Leah and Rachel. We've discovered both the power of envy and the power of contentment. Today we will wrap up our study by exploring the power of compassion in getting along with others.

Take a moment to open with prayer, and then invite the women to share what their name means. (Day 1, page 114). Allow the women to look up their names online if necessary. Remind the women of the importance of names in the Old Testament, as seen in the lives of Leah and Rachel.

Video (about 20 minutes)

Play the video segment for Week 4, filling in the blanks as you watch and making notes about anything that resonates with you or that you want to be sure to remember.

Group Session Guide:
WEEK 4

—Video Notes—

Key Scripture: Philippians 2:3

Selfless _____: "Do nothing out of selfless ambition"

Self-_____: "Do nothing out of . . . vain conceit"

_____: "In humility"

_____: "Value others above yourselves"

Other Insights:

Group Discussion (20–25 minutes for a 60-minute session; 30–35 minutes for a 90-minute session)

Video Discussion

- Read aloud Philippians 2:3. How would you explain this verse in your own words?
- Have you ever made something about you that wasn't about you at all? Share an example. What can help us to let go of selfish ambition and vain conceit and embrace self-effacement or humility instead? (Discuss the ways to foster humility named in the video and add your own to this list: spend time listening to others, focus on the present, be grateful, ask for help, seek feedback from others.)
- What does it mean to value others above yourself? What are some ways we can do this?
- What keeps us from losing ourselves or getting lost when we serve others?
- What do Rachel and Leah teach us about unhealthy competition? How might their story have been different if they had shown compassion for each other?

Group Session Guide:
WEEK 4

Workbook Discussion

- How can you leverage your advantages to help other people? (Day 1, page 117)
- Have you ever tried to manipulate a situation or take matters into your own hands because you grew impatient with God's timing or plans? What happened? (Day 2, page 122)
- On Day 2, you listed things the Lord has done for you in the last three months. Was any of those an answer to prayer? Was it answered on your schedule? Explain. (Day 2, page 123)
- On Day 3, you wrote down your desires at different ages. How have your desires changed over time? (Day 3, page 128)
- What outside influences lead you to feel discontent?
- What helps you live in contentment?
- Who has been your competition in the past? Did it ever get out of hand, leading to envy? If so, what was the result? (Day 4, page 135)
- How has God provided for your needs lately?
- When have you wrestled with God? What happened as a result? (Day 5, page 141)
- How would you define compassion?
- In what area of your life do you need to show more compassion? (coworkers, boss, spouse, children, yourself, others) (Day 5, page 143)
- What are some obstacles to showing compassion for others?

Connection Point (10–15 minutes—90-minute session only)

Divide into groups of two to three and discuss the following:

- If followers of Christ showed compassion for the plight of others, how would your community be different? How would our country be different? (Day 5, page 142)
- How might compassion be a key component in finding common ground with other people?

Closing Prayer (5 minutes)

Close the session by sharing personal prayer requests and praying together. If you like, invite the women to surround those who have shared requests and pray for them aloud. In addition to praying aloud for one another, close by asking God to help you become women who seek common ground with others as they strive to build deeper relationships that honor Him.

A Final Word

As I was writing this study, the world was in tumult as never before in my lifetime. A worldwide health crisis, a divisive election year, racial tension, panic, discord, name-calling, devastating fires, and increasing mental health issues made it seem that our disunity might cause ripples from which we might never recover. I searched the Scriptures for answers and insights and continued to be encouraged and challenged by the relationships between siblings we find in God's Word.

The sibling relationships and rivalries in the Bible provide an incredible opportunity to diagnose the pitfalls, problems, and pressures of living and working together as sisters and brothers in Christ. We are called to love one another (John 13:34-35) and live a life that reflects that love. The psalmist, David, remarks, "How good and pleasant it is / when God's people live together in unity!" (Psalm 133:1). Finding common ground with our siblings in Jesus is good and pleasant, indeed! But it also is *hard work* that requires commitment.

The first time we took our kids to Disneyland, my husband and I were way more excited than our kids were; they did not know what to expect. After checking in to the hotel the night before our day in the Magic Kingdom, we decided to go out for dinner; and as per our usual, we chose where to go based on a coupon I had collected. There is a fine line between cheap and financially wise, and I do backflips on that line every day.

This particular restaurant for which I had the coupon was super cool. The motif was jungle, and there were animatronic jungle animals all throughout the restaurant that would "come to life" about every thirty minutes. The first time the gorillas made noise and moved, both our kids burst into tears.

We had to appeal to their intellects to calm them down. We explained that they were not real gorillas but that computers inside the gorillas were controlling them. Our waitress explained that we could predict the next time the gorillas would be active because the sound of a rainstorm would precede the activity. When we heard the rain again, we held our kids' hands; but despite the warning, tears still welled up in their eyes. Our son, who was around five at the time, said, "Those computers are loud!"

The next morning when we entered the gates of Disneyland, I nearly lost my mind in excitement. The kids were dumbfounded at the sheer enormity of it all. We skipped through the park without a concern, laughing and pointing at all our eyes could see.

Then we saw our first character, Minnie Mouse, and the kids ran toward her as if pulled by a magnet. She waved at us and then crouched down to talk to a toddler. The toddler, overwhelmed by the magnitude of the Disney matriarch, burst into tears. Both of our kids comforted the wailing sample-sized cutie, saying, "It's okay, there is a computer inside her!"

The parents of that child shot a glance at our kids and then at us. They judged us for taking all the "magic" out of the Magic Kingdom. We realized that our kids had lost some of the wonder and mystery of the "fantasy" that day too.

Sometimes the idea of finding common ground might seem more like a fantasy than a reality, but the truth is that there's no mystery involved—or computers, for that matter! In fact, we have clear instructions in God's Word. Finding common ground takes trust in God, time in His Word, and practice; it requires humility and honor, prayer and pain, effort and education.

As we've learned from the lessons in our study, some of the specific ways we can love others despite our differences include:

- examining the eternal Word of God,
- seeking wisdom in the Scriptures in all seasons,
- trusting in God's truth,
- living to lead others to Christ,
- praying for peace,
- searching for strength in Christ,
- striving to strengthen others,
- putting aside pettiness,
- holding on to healing and forgiveness found only in Christ,
- practicing and seeking forgiveness with others,
- running toward reconciliation,
- calibrating for connection by being vulnerable, and
- embracing humility.

And in the process, by the grace of God, we will find common ground!

Leader Helps

Tips for Facilitating a Group

IMPORTANT INFORMATION

Before the first session you will want to distribute copies of this study guide to the members of your group. Be sure to communicate that, if possible, they are to complete the first week in the study guide *before* your first group session. For each week there are personal lessons divided into five sections, or days, which participants may choose to complete each day or all at once depending on their schedules and preferences.

As you gather each week with the members of your group, you will have the opportunity to watch a video, discuss and respond to what you're learning, and pray together. You will need access to a television and DVD player with working remotes or a computer and monitor if you will be viewing streaming video files (available from Cokesbury.com and Amplifymedia.com). Use the Group Session Guide at the end of each week's lessons to facilitate the session (options are provided for both a 60-minute and 90-minute meeting time). In addition to these guides, the Group Session Guide Leader Notes (pages 152–155) provide additional helps including a main objective, key Scripture references, and overview for each session.

Creating a warm and inviting atmosphere will help to make the women feel welcome. Although optional, you might consider providing snacks for your first meeting and inviting group members to rotate in bringing refreshments each week.

As group leader, your role is to guide and encourage the women on the journey to finding and thriving in their tribe and living in true biblical community. Pray that God would pour out His Spirit on your time together, that the Spirit would speak into each woman's life and circumstances, and that your group would grow in community with one another.

Preparing for the Sessions

- Be sure to communicate dates and times to participants in advance.
- Make sure that group members have their workbooks at least one week before your first session and instruct them to complete the first week of personal lessons in the study guide. If you have the phone numbers or email addresses of your group members, send out a reminder and a welcome.
- Check out your meeting space before each group session. Make sure the room is ready. Do you have enough chairs? Do you have the equipment and supplies you need? (See the list of materials that follows.)
- Pray for your group and each group member by name. Ask God to work in the life of every woman in your group.

- Read and complete the week's readings in this study guide and review the group session guide. Select the discussion points and questions you want to make sure to cover during your time together, as there will be more information here than you will likely be able to cover in your session. You might want to make notes in the margins to share in your discussion time.

LEADING THE SESSIONS

- Personally welcome and greet each woman as she arrives. Take attendance if desired.
- In order to create a warm, welcoming environment as the women are gathering, consider either lighting one or more candles, providing coffee or other refreshments, or playing worship music, or all of these. (Bring an iPod, smartphone, or tablet and a portable speaker if desired.) Be sure to provide name tags if the women do not know one another or you have new participants in your group.
- Always start on time. Honor the time of those who are on time.
- At the start of each session, ask the women to turn off or silence their cell phones.
- Communicate the importance of completing the weekly lessons and participating in group discussion.
- Encourage everyone to participate fully, but don't put anyone on the spot. Invite the women to share as they are comfortable. Be prepared to offer a personal example or answer if no one else responds at first.
- Facilitate but don't dominate. Remember that if you talk most of the time, group members may tend to listen rather than to engage. Your task is to encourage conversation and keep the discussion moving.
- If someone monopolizes the conversation, kindly thank her for sharing and ask if anyone else has any insights.
- Try not to interrupt, judge, or minimize anyone's comments or input.
- Remember that you are not expected to be the expert or have all the answers. Acknowledge that all of you are on this journey together, with the Holy Spirit as your leader and guide. If issues or questions arise that you don't feel equipped to handle, talk with the pastor or a staff member at your church.
- Don't rush to fill the silence. If no one speaks right away, it's okay to wait for someone to answer. After a moment, ask, "Would anyone be willing to share?" If no one responds, try asking the question again a different way, or offer a brief response and ask if anyone has anything to add.
- Encourage good discussion, but don't be timid about calling time on a particular question and moving ahead. Part of your responsibility is to keep the group on track. If you decide to spend extra time on a given question or activity, consider skipping or spending less time on another question or activity in order to stay on schedule.
- Do your best to end on time. If you are running over, give members the opportunity to leave if they need to. Then wrap up as quickly as you can.
- Thank the women for coming and let them know you're looking forward to seeing them next time.

- Be prepared for some women to want to hang out and talk at the end. If you need everyone to leave by a certain time, communicate this at the beginning of the group session. If you are meeting in a church during regularly scheduled activities, be aware of nursery closing times.

Materials Needed

- *Common Ground* study guide with leader helps
- *Common Ground* DVD and a DVD player, or a computer and monitor
- Stick-on name tags and markers (optional)
- iPod, smartphone, or tablet, and portable speaker (if desired for gathering music)

Group Session Guide Leader Notes

Use these notes for your own review and preparation. If desired, you can share the Main Objective, Key Scripture(s), and Overview with the group at the beginning of the session in order to set the tone for the session, as well as prepare everyone for content discussion, especially those who might have been unable to complete their personal lessons during the week.

Session 1: Joseph and His Brothers: Combating Jealousy

Main Objective

To recognize the destructive power of jealousy in our relationships and combat it by focusing on God's goodness in our lives

Key Scriptures

A heart at peace gives life to the body,
  but envy rots the bones.
        (Proverbs 14:30)

We demolish arguments and every pretension that sets itself up against the knowledge of God, and we take captive every thought to make it obedient to Christ.

(2 Corinthians 10:5)

Finally, brothers and sisters, whatever is true, whatever is noble, whatever is right, whatever is pure, whatever is lovely, whatever is admirable—if anything is excellent or praiseworthy—think about such things.

(Philippians 4:8)

The Advocate, the Holy Spirit, whom the Father will send in my name, will teach you all things and will remind you of everything I have said to you.

(John 14:26)

Overview

This week, we focused on the lives of Joseph and his brothers as a cautionary example of the powerful effects of jealousy. Talk about a dysfunctional family! We discovered how Joseph's father, Jacob, had singled out Joseph as his favorite son, causing disharmony among the brothers. Joseph made matters worse by telling his brothers about dreams in which he would rule over them. The contention between them led to the brothers selling Joseph into slavery in Egypt, telling their father that Joseph had died. God gave Joseph favor with his masters and Joseph was promoted to a high place. But because Joseph acted with integrity, he was thrown into prison.

Even through the worst of circumstances, God was with Joseph. When Joseph was able to interpret Pharaoh's dreams about an impending famine, Pharaoh promoted Joseph as second-in-command of the entire nation and charged Joseph with the task of preparing for the famine. And, because of the famine, Joseph's brothers went to Egypt to buy food; but they did not even recognize their own brother, who was in charge of distributing food. Joseph orchestrated a beautiful reunion in which he forgave his brothers and brought them under his protection during the famine.

The story of Joseph and his brothers shows us the destructive power of envy and jealousy, tearing apart a family and sending Joseph into exile in another country. The story also reveals the power of God at work, not only saving Joseph but also saving his relationship with his brothers. We watched as Joseph forgave his brothers and sought reconciliation rather than revenge. Joseph saw God as sovereign and trusted Him to bring good where evil had been at work.

We can follow Joseph's example, focusing on God's goodness and trusting His work in our lives. We can remind ourselves that God has not forgotten us—even in the darkest moments. We can leave the past in the past and allow God to create a new future for us. By keeping our eyes on God instead of the successes of others, we can avoid the pitfalls of envy and deepen our relationships with others.

Session 2: Moses, Miriam, and Aaron: Working Together Despite Differences

MAIN OBJECTIVE

To discover how to work together as uniquely equipped people to do the work God has called us to do rather than squabble about petty differences

KEY SCRIPTURE

[13]*Moses answered the people, "Do not be afraid. Stand firm and you will see the deliverance the LORD will bring you today. The Egyptians you see today you will never see again.* [14]*The LORD will fight for you; you need only to be still."*

(Exodus 14:13-14)

OVERVIEW

This week we examined the story of Moses, Miriam, and Aaron, whose lives span several chapters in the Bible. Their story begins in Exodus 2, when Moses's mother saved his life by hiding him in the reeds rather than obeying Pharaoh's edict to kill male babies. Moses's big sister, Miriam, looked after him until he was discovered by Pharaoh's daughter and eventually raised as Egyptian royalty. Years later, after killing an Egyptian for beating a Hebrew slave, Moses fled to the wilderness until God called him to lead the people of Israel out of Egypt and into freedom. God called Moses's siblings to help him complete this massive task. But their journey and their relationships were complicated and messy, which mirrors many of our relationships in daily life.

When Moses balked at being God's mouthpiece to Pharaoh, God called Aaron to help him. However, Aaron wasn't a perfect example either. He was a passive bystander when Moses acted out of anger toward the people (Exodus 17). And he caved to peer pressure and built a golden calf when

Moses stayed too long on the mountain with God (Exodus 32). On another occasion, both Aaron and Miriam grumbled against Moses (Numbers 12). These siblings were imperfect indeed.

However, Moses understood the need for other people. When the Israelites faced the Amalekites, he enlisted the help of Aaron and Hur (Moses's brother-in-law) to hold up his arms. And he listened to his father-in-law, Jethro, who encouraged Moses to set up a system of judges to deal with disputes among the people.

Their story is our story. We are imperfect. We doubt God and we grumble. We sometimes act in haste and frustration. We bow to peer pressure. Despite all of our failures and weaknesses, God still chooses to use us to accomplish great things. Just as these three grew in their leadership skills over time, so can we. And just as these three siblings learned to work together rather than squabble, we can learn to work with others, too.

Session 3: Mary, Martha, and Lazarus: *Appreciating the Contributions of Others*

MAIN OBJECTIVE

To focus on Jesus and draw attention to Him rather than become distracted by the situation or people around us

KEY SCRIPTURE:

⁴Just as each of us has one body with many members, and these members do not all have the same function, ⁵so in Christ we, though many, form one body, and each member belongs to all the others.

(Romans 12:4-5)

OVERVIEW

This week we looked into the lives of one of the most well-known group of siblings in Scripture—Mary, Martha, and Lazarus. We first met these three in Martha's home, where Mary and probably Lazarus listened to Jesus while Martha got distracted by making preparations. This story reminded us to focus on what's most important—a relationship with Jesus. Our work for Him should never replace our love and devotion to Him.

The next day of our study focused on Mary, who poured out perfume on Jesus's feet and then wiped His feet with her hair. While Judas was concerned with lining his own pockets, Mary was again focused on Jesus and her love for Him. Jesus praised Mary for her act of worship. And we discovered how Jesus saw the three siblings as more than the labels placed on them. Martha was more than a hostess and Lazarus was more than a guest at a dinner party. Jesus sees past the labels that others give us—and the labels we give ourselves.

We also looked at the most well-known encounter involving the three siblings, when Jesus went to the home of Mary and Martha after Lazarus's death (John 11). We saw each of the siblings as they encountered Jesus in unique ways. Martha saw Him as the Resurrection and the Life, while Mary gained encouragement as she cried out to Jesus for faith and understanding. And of course, Lazarus rose from the dead. This story was a reminder of the compassion of Jesus in the midst of our suffering. It also reminded us that God is weaving a story far beyond what we can imagine.

We wrapped up the week where we started—at the feet of Jesus in the home of Martha. This time, we saw how Martha's distraction, isolation, and anxiety kept her from experiencing fully what Jesus offered her, and we ended with a challenge to see how those emotions can keep us from Jesus, too.

Session 4: *Rachel and Leah*: Having Compassion for the Plight of Others

MAIN OBJECTIVE

To look past our own interests to see and meet the needs of others

KEY SCRIPTURE

Do nothing out of selfish ambition or vain conceit. Rather, in humility value others above yourselves.

(*Philippians* 2:3)

OVERVIEW

This week, we wrapped up our study by looking at the relationship between Leah and Rachel, two sisters who were vastly different in looks and personality, but who both found themselves at the mercy of their father's schemes. Their father, Laban, deceived Jacob (the original deceiver) into marrying his elder daughter, Leah, even though he was in love with the younger daughter, Rachel. We watched one sibling favored over the other, but we learned the importance of realizing how blessed we really are. We can use our advantages to help others and draw them to Jesus.

The relationship between Laban and Jacob continued to decline as the two tried to control their own destinies by manipulating and deceiving each other and their situations. While we might not understand their methods or reasons for their behavior, we can all relate to the desire to take control of situations instead of trusting God.

Even as the two men were trying to gain the upper hand, the sisters continued to compete for Jacob's affection by bearing children for him. While we don't face the same cultural biases they did, we understand their underlying motive. We are all tempted by the lie that "if only" we had a certain thing (spouse, child, job, and so on), then we would be content. The cycle of "more" can derail the best relationships. The truth is that our hearts will always be discontent apart from God.

Eventually, Jacob left with both wives and returned to his homeland, where he and his brother, Esau, eventually reconciled with each other. God brought healing to a tattered relationship, which gives us hope for our fractured friendships.

This week showed us how personal ambition can damage relationships. It highlighted the problem of seeking after something to give us fulfillment when only God can ultimately make us whole. And we discovered how God can bring blessing out of heartache, even those places that seem void of any hope. He is always working for our good and His glory.

VIDEO NOTE ANSWERS

Week 1
life / rots
Recapture
Refocus
Remind

Week 2
Community
Command
Conquest
Choice

Week 3
Members
Strength / satisfaction / success / self-control
function
Savior
belonging

Week 4
ambition
effacement
service

Notes

Week 1

1. James Montgomery Boice, *Genesis: An Expositional Commentary*. (Grand Rapids: Baker Publishing Group, 1998), NA. Quoted in *Enduring Word Commentary*, https://enduringword.com/bible-commentary/genesis-37/, accessed December 2, 2020.

2. Robert Jamieson, A. R. Fausset, and David Brown, "A Commentary, Critical, Practical, and Explanatory on the Old and New Testaments, 1882," Bible Hub, https://biblehub.com/commentaries/jfb/genesis/37.htm, accessed December 2, 2020.

3. "Genesis 37," *The Pulpit Commentary*, Bible Hub, https://biblehub.com/commentaries/pulpit/genesis/37.htm, accessed December 2, 2020.

4. Fred H. Wight, "Shepherd Life: The Care of Sheep and Goats," from Manners and Customs of Bible Lands, Ancient Hebrew Research Center, https://www.ancient-hebrew.org/manners/shepherd-life-the-care-of-sheep-and-goats.htm, accessed December 2, 2020.

5. "Joseph," BBC, Religions, https://www.bbc.co.uk/religion/religions/judaism/history/joseph.shtml, accessed December 3, 2020.

6. "I am with you," New International Bible, https://www.biblegateway.com/quicksearch/?quicksearch=i+am+with+you&version=NIV, accessed December 3, 2020.

7. *The Enduring Word Bible Commentary*, "Genesis 41.Joseph Interprets Pharaoh's Dream and Rises to Power," https://enduringword.com/bible-commentary/genesis-41/, accessed December 3, 2020.

8. David Guzik, "Study Guide for Genesis 41," *Blue Letter Bible*, https://www.blueletterbible.org/Comm/guzik_david/StudyGuide2017-Gen/Gen-41.cfm?a=41001, accessed December 3, 2020.

9. Guzik, "Study Guide for Genesis 41," accessed December 3, 2020.

10. Footnote f, https://www.biblegateway.com/passage/?search=Genesis+41&version=NIV, accessed December 3, 2020.

11. Dr. Thomas Constable, "Commentary on Genesis 42:4," Expository Notes of Dr. Thomas Constable, StudyLight, https://www.studylight.org/commentaries/dcc/genesis-42.html.

12. Encyclopedia Britannica, s.v., "Pharaoh," revised and updated by Adam Augustyn, https://www.britannica.com/topic/pharaoh, accessed December 3, 2020.

13. Constable, "Commentary on Genesis 42:4," accessed December 3, 2020.

Week 2

1. Robert Jamieson, A. R. Fausset, and David Brown, "Commentary on Exodus 2," *Blue Letter Bible*, https://www.blueletterbible.org/Comm/jfb/Exd/Exd_002.cfm?a=52002, accessed December 4, 2020.

2. Encyclopedia of the Bible, s.v. "Priests and Levites," https://www.biblegateway.com/resources/encyclopedia-of-the-bible/Priests-Levites, accessed December 4, 2020.

3. Oxford English and Spanish Dictionary, s.v. "Illusion," https://www.lexico.com/en/definition/illusion, accessed December 4, 2020.

4. "Nobody's Perfect," written by Matthew Gerrard and Robbie Nevil, performed by Miley Cyrus as Hannah Montana, https://www.lyrics.com/lyric/30025072/Miley+Cyrus/Nobody's+Perfect, accessed December 4, 2020.

5. Adam Clarke, "Commentary on Numbers 20:12," *The Adam Clarke Commentary*, StudyLight, https://www.studylight.org/commentaries/acc/numbers-20.html, accessed December 4, 2020.

6. David Guzik, "Study Guide for Numbers 20," *Blue Letter Bible*, https://www.blueletterbible.org/Comm/guzik_david/StudyGuide2017-Num/Num-20.cfm?a=137002, accessed December 5, 2020.

7. Albert Barnes, "Commentary on Numbers 12:4," *Barnes' Notes on the Whole Bible*, StudyLight, https://www.studylight.org/commentaries/bnb/numbers-12.html, accessed December 5, 2020.

8. John Wesley, "Commentary on Numbers 12:4," *John Wesley's Explanatory Notes on the Whole Bible*, StudyLight, https://www.studylight.org/commentaries/wen/numbers-12.html, accessed December 5, 2020.

9. "All the Women of the Bible," Biblegateway.com, https://www.biblegateway.com/devotionals/all-women-bible/5641/10/28, accessed December 5, 2020.

10. "Dream Team 25 Years," https://www.foxsports.com.au/basketball/dream-team-25-years-us-olympic-legends-killed-in-littleremembered-scrimmage-against-college-stars/news-story/87db9f49545331f6eae8974be6484688, accessed December 5, 2020.

11. "Dream Team 25 Years."

12. Josh Howgego, "Honeybees Gang Up to Roast Invading Hornets Alive—at a Terrible Cost," *NewScientist*, https://www.newscientist.com/article/2174097-honeybees-gang-up-to-roast-invading-hornets-alive-at-a-terrible-cost/, accessed December 5, 2020.

Week 3

1. Charles Pope, "What Were Weddings Like in Jesus' Day?" *Catholic Standard*, https://cathstan.org/posts/what-were-weddings-like-in-jesus-day-2, accessed December 6, 2020.

2. Marg Mowczko, "Mary, Martha and Lazarus of Bethany," https://margmowczko.com/martha-mary-and-lazarus-of-bethany/, accessed December 6, 2020.

3. E. W. G. Masterman, "Bethany," Bible Hub, https://bibleatlas.org/bethany.htm, accessed December 6, 2020.

4. Erin McDowell, "18 of the Most Epic Sibling Rivalries of All Time," *Business Insider*, https://www.businessinsider.com/famous-sibling-rivalries-2014-6#advice-columnists-and-twin-sisters-eppie-lederer-and-pauline-phillips-feuded-over-their-respective-and-identical-columns-15, accessed December 6, 2020.

5. Kindalee Pfremmer DeLong, "Women and Culture in the New Testament World," *Leaven* 4, Spring 1996, https://digitalcommons.pepperdine.edu/cgi/viewcontent.cgi?article=1894&context=leaven, accessed December 6, 2020.

6. Mary Jane Chaignot, "Mary and Martha," *BibleWise*, https://www.biblewise.com/bible_study/characters/mary-martha.php. Accessed December 6, 2020.

7. *Bible History*, s.v. "Tables,", https://www.bible-history.com/links.php?cat=39&sub=477&cat_name=Manners+&+Customs&subcat_name=Eating+Customs, accessed December 7, 2020.

8. Gerlyn Hollingsworth, "On This day: Reclining at Table," *National Catholic Reporter*, https://www.ncronline.org/blogs/ncr-today/day-reclining-table, accessed December 7, 2020.

9. Dr. William Smith, "Entry for 'Spikenard'" *Smith's Bible Dictionary*, 1901, https://www.biblestudytools.com/dictionaries/smiths-bible-dictionary/spikenard.html, accessed December 7, 2020.

10. "What Is Spikenard in the Bible?" Got Questions, https://www.gotquestions.org/spikenard-in-the-Bible.html, accessed December 7, 2020.

11. Mary Jane Chaignot, "Mary and Martha," *Bible Wise*, https://www.biblewise.com/bible_study/characters/mary-martha.php, accessed December 7, 2020.

12. William Barclay, "Commentary on John 12:4," *William Barclay's Daily Study Bible*, 1956–59, StudyLight, https://www.studylight.org/commentaries/dsb/john-12.html, 1956–59, accessed December 7, 2020.

13. "Ephesians 1," *Expositor's Bible Commentary*, https://biblehub.com/commentaries/expositors/ephesians/1.htm, accessed December 7, 2020.

14. "Statistics in the Ministry," Pastoral Care Inc., https://www.pastoralcareinc.com/statistics/, accessed December 7, 2020.
15. Kelly Gooch, "Study: 92% of Nurses Report Moderate to Very High Stress Levels," *Becker's Hospital Review*, https://www.beckershospitalreview.com/hr/study-92-of-nurses-report-moderate-to-very-high-stress-levels.html, accessed December 7, 2020.
16. Bourree Lam, "The Dangerous Life of a Trash Collector," *The Atlantic*, https://www.theatlantic.com/business/archive/2016/09/trash-collector/498233/, accessed December 7, 2020.
17. Matthew Tull, "Development of PTSD in Firefighters," *Verywell Mind*, https://www.verywellmind.com/rates-of-ptsd-in-firefighters-2797428#:~:text=Given%20that%20traumatic%20exposure%20is,a%20current%20diagnosis%20of%20PTSD, accessed December 7, 2020.
18. Jenny Grant Rankin, "The Teacher Burnout Epidemic, Part 1of 2," *Psychology Today*, https://www.psychologytoday.com/us/blog/much-more-common-core/201611/the-teacher-burnout-epidemic-part-1-2, accessed December 7, 2020.
19. Courtney Lund O'Neil, "Stay-at-Home-Mom Depression Is Real—And You're Not Alone," Parents.com, https://www.parents.com/parenting/moms/stay-at-home-mom-depression-is-real/, accessed December 7, 2020.
20. https://biblehub.com/commentaries/cambridge/luke/10.htm, accessed December 7, 2020.
21. "Luke 10:40," *The Interlinear Bible*, Bible Hub, https://biblehub.com/interlinear/luke/10-40.htm, accessed December 7, 2020.

Week 4

1. "Two Brothers, Two Sneakers, and a Global Battle for Footwear," *Sports History Weekly*, https://sportshistoryweekly.com/stories/adidas-puma-sports-sneakers-kleats,658, accessed December 7, 2020.
2. *Pulpit Commentary*, Bible Hub, https://biblehub.com/commentaries/pulpit/genesis/29-16.htm, accessed December 7, 2020.
3. *Ellicott's Commentary for English Readers*, Bible Hub, https://biblehub.com/commentaries/genesis/29-16.htm, accessed December 7, 2020.
4. Robert Jamieson, "Commentary on Genesis 29," *Blue Letter Bible*, https://www.blueletterbible.org/Comm/jfb/Gen/Gen_029.cfm?a=29001, accessed December 7, 2020.
5. Natasha Burton, "Most Women Don't Feel Beautiful," *Cosmopolitan*, https://www.cosmopolitan.com/style-beauty/beauty/news/a11997/most-women-dont-think-theyre-beautiful/#:~:text=Well%2C%20that's%20just%20depressing!,has%20something%20beautiful%20about%20her, accessed December 7, 2020.
6. Jana Aneles, "Education Statistics around the Globe," *Upskilled*, https://www.upskilled.edu.au/skillstalk/education-statistics-around-the-globe, accessed December 7, 2020.
7. "Poverty," The World Bank, https://www.worldbank.org/en/topic/poverty/overview, accessed February 3, 2021.
8. "World Health Statistics," World Health Organization, https://www.who.int/health-statistics, accessed December 7, 2020.
9. "Has Everyone Heard?" The Joshua Project, https://joshuaproject.net/resources/articles/has_everyone_heard, accessed December 7, 2020.
10. Linda Spencer, "Why Socks Are So Important to the Homeless," Community West Foundation, https://www.communitywestfoundation.org/blog/infographic-why-socks-are-so-important-to-the-homeless, accessed December 7, 2020.
11. James D. G. Dunn, ed., *Eerdmans Commentary on the Bible* (Grand Rapids,: Wm. B. Eerdmans Publishing, 2003), 59.
12. Bible Hub, s.v. "Mandrakes,", https://biblehub.com/topical/m/mandrakes.htm#amt, accessed December 8, 2020.

13. "Knocking at Your Back Door," https://www.lyricfind.com/. Songwriters Ian Gillan / Ritchie Blackmore / Roger D. Glover. Knocking at Your Back Door lyrics © BMG Rights Management.

14. Kathy Lipp, *The Clutter-Free Home: Making Room for Your Life* (Eugene, OR: Harvest House Publishers, 2020), 21.

15. Katie Serena, "Mary Boleyn—the Other Boleyn Girl Who Wooed Henry VIII," *All That's Interesting*, https://allthatsinteresting.com/mary-boleyn, accessed December 8, 2020.

16. Lauren Puckett, "The True Story Behind the Schuyler Sisters in Hamilton," *Harper's Bazaar*, https://www.harpersbazaar.com/culture/film-tv/a33094097/hamilton-schuyler-sisters-true-story/, accessed December 8, 2020.

17. Joseph J. Ellis, *Founding Brothers: The Revolutionary Generation* (New York: Knopf Doubleday Publishing Group, 2003), 163.

18. Ellis, *Founding Brothers*, 222.

19. Ellis, *Founding Brothers*, 220.

20. Ellis, *Founding Brothers*, 223, and endnote 32 on page 276 (for date of letter).

21. Ellis, *Founding Brothers*, 248.

22. Robert Jamieson, "Commentary on Genesis 31," *Commentary Critical and Explanatory on the Whole Bible, Blue Letter Bible*, https://www.blueletterbible.org/Comm/jfb/Gen/Gen_031.cfm?a=31004, accessed December 8, 2020.

23. *Baker's Evangelical Dictionary of Biblical Theology*, s.v., "Israel," Bible Study Tools, https://www.biblestudytools.com/dictionary/israel/, accessed December 8, 2020.

24. "The Twelve Tribes," My Jewish Learning, https://www.myjewishlearning.com/article/the-twelve-tribes/, accessed December 8, 2020.

Printed in the USA
CPSIA information can be obtained
at www.ICGtesting.com
LVHW081509130524
779771LV00001B/1